JELLY ROLL, JABBO, AND FATS

BOOKS BY WHITNEY BALLIETT

The Sound of Surprise
Dinosaurs in the Morning
Such Sweet Thunder
Super-Drummer: A Profile of Buddy Rich
Ecstasy at the Onion
Alec Wilder and His Friends
New York Notes
Improvising
American Singers
Night Creature
Jelly Roll, Jabbo, and Fats

Jelly Roll, Jabbo, and Fats

19 Portraits in Jazz

Whitney Balliett

NEW YORK   OXFORD UNIVERSITY PRESS   1983

Most of the material in this book appeared in
somewhat different form in *The New Yorker* magazine.

Library of Congress Cataloging in Publication Data

Balliett, Whitney.
   Jelly Roll, Jabbo, and Fats.

   1. Jazz musicians—Addresses, essays, lectures.
2. Jazz music—Addresses, essays, lectures.   I. Title.
ML3507.B35   1983   785.42'092'2   82-22557
ISBN 0-19-503275-6 (Cloth)

Printing (last digit): 9 8 7 6 5 4 3 2 1

Printed in the United States of America

For Susan Moritz

Note

This book was written over the past seven years, and it deals with two French jazz critics, six pianists, four saxophonists, three drummers, two trumpeters, one trombonist, and one bassist. The oldest player, Jelly Roll Morton, was born in 1890, and the youngest, Michael Moore, in 1945, so the book, like my earlier *Improvising*, can be read as a loose history of the music. The French critics—Hugues Panassié and Charles Delaunay—are here because their ministrations, carried on an ocean away in the thirties and forties, had much to do with alerting this country to the fact that it had a new and beautiful music at its door.

New York City   W.B.
September 1982

Contents

JELLY ROLL, JABBO, AND FATS

Panassié, Delaunay et Cie

A singular work of musical criticism was published in France in 1934. It was called "Le Jazz Hot," and it was written by a twenty-two-year-old Frenchman named Hugues Panassié. Aside from the erratic "Aux Frontières du Jazz," brought out two years before by the Belgian Robert Goffin, it was the first book of jazz criticism, and it put jazz on the map in Europe and in its own country—an English translation was published here in 1936 as "Hot Jazz"—where the music had been ignored or misunderstood for its entire forty-year life. (The French are old hands at introducing other cultures to themselves. Edmund Wilson often spoke of how much Taine's "Histoire de la Littérature Anglaise" had influenced him, to say nothing of the English.) "Hot Jazz" is a passionate work. Panassié had found what he believed to be the most beautiful music in the world, and his book rings with superlatives and clarion bursts. He writes of the Chicago clarinettist Frank Teschemacher, who was killed in an auto accident in 1932:

I can here give you no idea of the power in his execution, that overflowing ardor, that lyric eloquence which gives Teschemacher's solos such expressive force. . . . There is another marvellous thing about Teschemacher: his intonations are so beautiful that they alone move me profoundly.

Of Mary Lou Williams:

Her style derives from the James P. Johnson and Fats Waller style, but is much more fantastic and ardent. On "Night Life" she has made one of the most beautiful hot piano solo records we have. Her hot, panting right-hand phrases, and the swing she gets by the accentuations in the bass by the left hand, must both be admired.

Of Coleman Hawkins:

Since the end of 1932, Hawkins has devised . . . a style almost entirely free from Armstrong influence. Those violent, villainous phrases, with their steel structures and their tragic import, are gone; instead, there are melodic curves of exquisite charm, full of a sweet sadness, although his intonations have not lost their sombre force.

All first-rate criticism defines *what* we are encountering, and Panassié, revealing an uncommon perspicacity—his book is based almost wholly on phonograph recordings—organizes the music into appropriate schools, grades the performers on each instrument, gives a chapter to Duke Ellington, one to other big bands, and one to big-band arrangers, and attempts to explain the mysteries of improvisation and swinging. He was writing about musicians who as often as not were still neophytes. He marvels at Art Tatum when Tatum had hardly begun recording; at Sidney Catlett, then twenty-three and also hardly recorded; at Duke Ellington, who would not be celebrated in his own country for many years; at Bix Beiderbecke's beautiful (and often maligned) last recordings; and at the pioneer rhythmic excellences of Luis Russell's 1930 band. Panassié, working three thousand miles from his subject, unavoidably stumbles here and there. He voices his inexplicable (and lifelong) admiration for the abysmal clarinettist Mezz Mezzrow. He scants the great Red Allen. He places the simplistic trumpeter Tommy Ladnier next to Louis Armstrong. He overpraises the Chicago school. (See Teschemacher.) He gets his musical antecedents crossed up. (Jack Teagarden did not come out of Jimmy Harrison; Teagarden was all there when he arrived in New York in 1927.) He gets involved in interminable lists of supposedly promising but unkown musicians who remain unknown forty years later. But "Hot Jazz" was a revolutionary cele-bration, and it turned on the first generation of jazz lis-teners.

Panassié's next book to be published here, "The Real Jazz," appeared in 1942 and was revised in 1960. (In all, he wrote more than a dozen books—including his six-hundred-page "Summing Up," which came out in France in 1958 and was called "Discographie Critique des Meilleurs Disques de Jazz"—but only five of them have been published in the United States.) It is a reworking of "Hot Jazz," and it dem-onstrates that Panassié ceased all forward critical motion around 1940, when he was just twenty-eight. (There are exceptions in "The Real Jazz," for he is startlingly correct about the budding Ray Charles, and about Lester Young. "There is something dreamy about Lester," he writes, "a nonchalant accent in the execution which makes his music seem as if it were spoken confidentially to each of his lis-teners.") He had also come down with Mezzrow fever, a Kafkaesque ailment that causes white men to long to be black, and accordingly he all but dumped the Chicago school, dismissing Beiderbecke and Pee Wee Russell and Joe Venuti and Jess Stacy, and either brushing past or ignoring com-pletely such younger white musicians as Zoot Sims, Eddie Costa, Buddy De Franco, Gerry Mulligan, Tal Farlow, Jimmy Raney, Stan Getz, and Serge Chaloff. Worst of all—in an icy stroke of critical perversity—he declares bebop un-constitutional. It is, he concludes in "Guide to Jazz," which was published here in 1956, a "form of music distinct from jazz because: (1) its players have abandoned the classic in-strumental jazz tradition. Instead of making their instruments sing like the human voice with inflections, vibrato, sustained notes and phrases full of contrast [a perfect description of Charlie Parker], the boppers play according to the European instrumental tradition; (2) because the bop rhythm section breaks the continuity of the swing . . . (3) because boppers systematically use chords and intervals adopted from modern European music and destroy the harmonic atmosphere of jazz." So avaunt, Parker, Dizzy Gillespie, Bud Powell, Thelonious Monk, Max Roach, Fats Navarro, and even his once beloved Mary Lou Williams, whom he accuses of turning to bop.

Panassié, riding the momentum of his great originality in "Hot Jazz," inevitably became messianic. He believed he could alter—or at least slow down—the course of jazz, and in 1938 he tried. He came to this country and organized four recording sessions for RCA Victor, which were released on its subsidiary Bluebird label. Three of the sessions presaged the New Orleans revival, which got under way in 1940 and came to a climax in 1947, when Bunk Johnson, hoary and drunken and mythicized, appeared at Stuyvesant Casino. Panassié used, in various combinations, Tommy Ladnier, whom he pried out of retirement, Sidney Bechet, Sidney de Paris, James P. Johnson, and the ubiquitous Mezzrow. The records attempted to re-create the classic collective improvisations at the heart of New Orleans jazz, and one reason that they faltered is suggested by Sidney Bechet in his autobiography, "Treat It Gentle":

> The men were supposed to be [at Panassié's record date] pretty early in the morning. But something had got going the night before and when they showed up at the studio they were really out. . . . Tommy [Ladnier] showed up dead drunk. James P. Johnson, he just stretched himself on the piano and passed out. Some of the musicianers didn't know how many fingers they'd got on each hand. But they went ahead and recorded somehow. And after it had all been cut Tommy knew the records weren't what they could have been and he wanted to say something to appease Panassié, who was sitting in the corner holding his head. . . . So he

pulled himself up and called out "*Vive la France!*," and then almost fell flat on his face.

Panassié also organized a somewhat more modern date, which included Frankie Newton, Pete Brown, James P., Al Casey, John Kirby, Cozy Cole, and Mezzrow. Newton is in top form, particularly in his long, crooning, muted solo on "The Blues My Baby Gave to Me," and so is Pete Brown, the mighty three-hundred-pound alto saxophonist whose telegraphic phrases swung so hard. His fast solos jump and stomp here, and his slow ones, particularly on the blues, hum indivisibly and admiringly alongside the beat. Eddie Condon, who hadn't been invited to participate, issued a mot on Panassié's visit: "I don't see why we need a Frenchman to come over here and tell us how to play American music. I wouldn't think of going to France and telling him how to jump on a grape."

Panassié, who died in 1975, at the age of sixty-two, had an invaluable alter ego during his best days. He is a small, gentle, sad man named Charles Delaunay, and, aside from having been Panassié's sidekick, he has done three inestimable things for jazz: with Panassié he started *Jazz Hot*, now the world's oldest pure jazz magazine; with Panassié he organized the peerless Paris recordings built around Django Reinhardt, Eddie South, Dicky Wells, Rex Stewart, Bill Coleman, and Barney Bigard; and he published, in 1948, "New Hot Discography," the first comprehensive work of its kind. It is a wonder, though, that Delaunay accomplished anything at all, for he was the only child of Sonia and Robert Delaunay—non-stop, teeming geometric painters, who took up a lot of room not only in their own house but in the Paris art world of the teens and twenties and thirties. Gertrude Stein was ambivalent about Robert Delaunay. (Sonia, who was for decades an extremely successful designer, did not make her mark as a painter until the early fifties.) Stein wrote to a friend in 1912, "We have not seen much of the Delaunays lately. There is a feud on. He wanted to wean

Apollinaire and me from liking Picasso and there was a great deal of amusing intrigue . . . Now Delaunay does conceive himself as a great solitaire and as a matter of fact he is an incessant talker and will tell all about himself and his value at any hour of the day or night." She continued to vacillate in "The Autobiography of Alice B. Toklas":

> Delaunay was a big blond frenchman . . . [who] was fairly able and inordinately ambitious. He was always asking how old Picasso had been when he had painted a certain picture. When he was told he always said, oh I am not as old as that yet. I will do as much when I am that age.
>
> As a matter of fact he did progress very rapidly. He used to come a great deal to the rue de Fleurus. Gertrude Stein used to delight in him. He was funny and he painted one rather fine picture, the three graces standing in front of Paris, an enormous picture in which he combined everybody's ideas and added a certain french clarity and freshness of his own. It had a rather remarkable atmosphere and it had a great success. After that his pictures lost all quality, they grew big and empty or small and empty. I remember his bringing one of these small ones to the house, saying, look I am bringing you a small picture, a jewel. It is small, said Gertrude Stein, but is it a jewel.

Delaunay *fils*—gray-haired, with Malraux features—talked one afternoon in May in New York about his life. He had not visited the city for twenty-seven years. He talked slowly, in a low and distant voice, a voice that barely sustained his words. At the end of the afternoon, he inscribed a copy of his discography in gossamer handwriting that echoes his speech: it has become so microscopic that he himself has difficulty reading it.

On How He Came to Love le Jazz Hot: "I first heard jazz when I was fifteen. I happened to be sick, staying six months in bed. My parents had fifty records altogether, and three were jazz—Jelly Roll Morton's 'Black Bottom Stomp,' Duke Ellington's 'East St. Louis Toodle-oo,' and a Frankie Trumbauer with Bix Beiderbecke. The 'Black Bottom' sounded like country dance music, like folklore. I would study what the cornet was playing and then what the clarinet was playing and then what the trombone was playing, and little by little these three came together clearly. Being a jazz lover in Paris in the twenties was like being an early Christian in Rome. I thought I was the only one interested. When I mentioned jazz in school, they'd say, 'Hey! *Alors!* That is nothing—just some Negro music.' But other people listened, and by 1933, when I finished my military service, two students had formed the Hot Club of France. Maybe we had heard three hundred records in Paris, and every time a new one came into a record shop on the Place de l'Opéra the phone was ringing and we'd all get together to listen. Even to have a flyer about an upcoming record—that was precious. We heard our first real jazz musicians at the Ambassadeurs, where Sam Wooding and Noble Sissle played. On summer days, you could hear the music out in the gardens, and you could climb a tree and see the whole band through a window. A musician who helped us was Freddy Johnson, the piano player with Sam Wooding. He was a grand player, but, more important, he was a jazz lover. He taught French musicians, like Alix Combelle, to play, and he taught us how to tell the difference on Fletcher Henderson records between the trumpet players Joe Smith and Tommy Ladnier and Rex Stewart. It was difficult to identify soloists before that. We learned the history of jazz through his words. Then a lot of American jazz musicians started arriving in Paris. Benny Carter came in 1934 or 1935, and most of the English I have now is from him. *Alors,* it was like being in church to meet jazz musicians. We were scared, and it was hard to get a mutual understanding. I met Louis Armstrong in 1934, and I took Django Reinhardt with me. Louis had made some concerts in England, and I think he had some trouble with his lip. So he was like a tourist on vacation in Paris. It was summer, and when we went to see Louis, he was half naked and had a stocking on his head, and he was already getting fat. He was shaving, and after a while I said to him, 'May I ask Django to play?' Well, I knew what Django's dream was, because he told me so many times, 'If Louis would hear me, he would take me to America, where I would be the guest of Clark Gable and play for the Hollywood stars right by their pools.' Django had brought his brother Joseph on rhythm guitar, and they started playing. Louis was still shaving, and every once in a while he would grunt, and when Django and Joseph finished, Louis was washing his face, and he only said, 'Yeh, not bad, man.' And that was all. It was the only time I ever saw Django, who always had a very good opinion of his own playing, looking absolutely blank. Duke Ellington came the first time in 1933, and he gave three concerts at the Salle Pleyel. It was *électrique*. It was the first time we heard a band like that, with all the mutes and the strange rhythms. The hall was packed, even though most of the people did not know what they were hearing. I got to know Ellington in 1939, when he made his second European tour. He was a personality that found everything so pleasant, so interesting. He was full of those small attentions that give you a good feeling. He behaved to everyone like a man who is in love."

On Jazz in Paris During and After the Second World War: "Jazz became popular in France when the Germans came. Suddenly we couldn't have American movies or American records anymore, and it was a shock, like when you stop smoking. French jazz musicians who had no reputation three weeks before became famous. Musicians all became swing cats and wore long coats and thick shoes. Jazz records—the ones that were left—began to sell. Some Germans even liked the music. One night, a German officer, very polite, very *apologétique*, came to the Rue Chaptal, where we published *Jazz Hot*, and asked if we minded if he played our piano. He sat down and played and sang Fats Waller for an hour, and when he finished, he thanked us and said that made him feel much better. The first band to come to Paris after the war belonged to Don Redman. The stores in Paris did not start getting American records again until 1948, and some of the first were by Dizzy Gillespie and Charlie Parker on the Guild label—'Shaw 'Nuff' and 'Salt Peanuts' and 'Hot House' and 'Groovin' High.' Those records were playing day and night at the Rue Chaptal. Everybody was saying, What is happening? What is that chord? How can he play so fast? What is happening in this music? It created an unbelievable sensation, and when Dizzy Gillespie's big band gave a concert the next year, the same amazement took place. That concert happened in this way: I was informed somehow that Dizzy's big band was stranded in Antwerp without a damn penny. So we got together some money and sent it to Antwerp, and we organized a concert for the band to give in Paris. The band arrived at nine-thirty at night and got onstage at ten-thirty. The band was starving, but something happened on that stage—just like with Duke Ellington in 1933—and the band made such a success it stayed in Paris one month and worked the whole time."

On His Record-Making Days: "I started directing record dates in 1934, when I did Reinhardt's and Stéphane Grappelli's first records together. Then I organized my Swing label and recorded Grappelli and Django and Eddie South and Bill Coleman. When Teddy Hill was in Paris in 1937, I took three of his trumpeters—Coleman and Shad Collins and Bill Dillard—and Dicky Wells and put them with Django plus a rhythm section, and we made 'Bugle Call Rag' and 'Between the Devil and the Deep Blue Sea.' The fourth trumpeter that Hill had, and I did not use, was Dizzy Gillespie, who was just nineteen. What a pity! After the war, I recorded Grappelli and Django again. Their first meeting was in London, where Grappelli had spent the war. They couldn't say anything except 'Mon frère, mon frère,' and the first thing they played was 'La Marseillaise.' In 1949, I brought Sidney Bechet over from America and also Charlie Parker and Miles Davis and Max Roach and Tadd Dameron and Kenny Dorham and Hot Lips Page. When Parker heard

Bechet, he was astonished. 'Hey, that old man can blow,' he said. 'He's playing things I thought I did first.' I don't know how peasants are in America, but in France they are concrete, solid, no abstractions. They know how things are growing. Bechet was like that. He would talk to anyone on the street. He had that accent that connected with everybody. He played all the time, and he packed all the halls. He became a living legend in France. His records would sell three hundred thousand copies each, and many broke the one-million mark, which is a lot in a country that has only fifty million people."

On Django Reinhardt: "There were two personalities in him. One was primitive. He never went to school and he couldn't stand a normal bed. He had to live in a gypsy caravan near a river, where he could fish and catch trout between the stones with his bare hands, and where he could put laces between the trees and catch rabbits. But Django also had a nobility, even though he could be very mean to the musicians who worked for him. Life for Django was all music. He was full of constant enthusiasm when he played—shouting in the record studio when someone played something he liked, shouting when he played himself. You can hear him on 'Bugle Call Rag.' When he was accompanying in the bass register he sounded like brass, and in the treble like saxophones. He had a constant vision of music—a circle of music—in his head. I think he could *see* his music. This way, he composed some music for symphony orchestra. He would play it on his guitar, all the parts—for flutes, for strings, for horns—and someone would write it down, and when you heard the piece, it was perfect. There were some waves of Ravel and Debussy, but the rest was Django. Of course, Django had a terrible cicatrix on his left hand. He had been in a fire and two fingers were bent into his palm. So, with him, it was the rapidity of his reactions to the music around him which made him sound so fast. Later, it became a goal for him to play the electric guitar, to dominate the electricity. He died of a stroke after an afternoon of fishing, which was the perfect ending for Django."

On His Beginnings: "I was born January 18, 1911. My father was like an open window. He was Gallic, and he had *la force de la nature*. He was speaking a lot and he was moving a lot. When he was caught by his painting, he would go to his atelier every day from six in the morning until nine at night to catch the last drop of light. And he would be in a very bad humor most of the time. He would be exhausted after only sleeping half the night, worrying about what he was going to paint the next day. He would work and work and work on the same idea, and then suddenly he would stop painting, and not paint again for several months. My father was living in dreams. He would say he was going to build big houses so he could paint big walls. After he went through the Cubist time, his only patience was with colors, with the relations of colors to one another. It became a religion of color to him, an obsession. He was like a chemist: what happens to one color when another color is brought together with it. My mother was more with her feet on the earth. She is much quieter—she is ninety-one and lives in Paris and still paints—and my father found some stability in her. I think they influenced each other as painters. They had some money until the first war; then my mother did very well with her designing. She designed everything—car seats, dresses, scarves, playing cards, rugs, tapestries, stained-glass windows, wigs. After my father died, in 1941, she devoted ten years to making him famous. I think when I was growing up I must have seen fifty per cent of all the well-known people in Paris passing in and out of our apartment—Apollinaire and Kandinski and Stravinsky and Diaghilev and Klee and Mondrian and Breton and Aragon. Of course, in Paris before the war everybody used to meet in the cafés and in their homes. They discussed art. They discussed music. They discussed books. They discussed each other. They discussed all night. Paris was filled with talking before the war. But after the war that all went, and now no one meets anymore. They did not pay attention to me, my parents, even though I was an only child. But things went all right. I did not go to the university, because when the time came I was already drawing ads and making a living at it. I didn't like modern art—what my parents did. I became an Impressionist painter, and my father used to say to me, 'Oh, you're just an old-fashioned guy.' "

On His Great Discography: "The first edition of my discography came about this way. To begin with, I probably had a hundred records in my collection, and, of course, in the twenties and thirties there was almost no information on the label about who was playing or when and where the record was made. Freddy Johnson helped us, and when musicians like Benny Carter started coming to Paris, I took a turntable to their rooms and played records and they helped us with the soloist. I put together a small booklet of personnels, because people were worrying me all the time for information, and I published it in *Jazz Hot*. Then in 1936 we put out the first discography in book form. After the war, I started writing the record companies over here, and then I came over and discovered I could find much information from the union sheets. My discography is still around, but Brian Rust and Jepsen are more complete and up to date—for now, anyway. I am one of more than twenty discographers who are putting together a new discography, starting in 1942 and coming down to the present. It will take about twenty thousand pages. It is incredible. When the volumes come out, they will be already out of date, but you can't do anything about that. Now my record collection has grown to perhaps thirty thousand items, which is nothing when Mr. Bob Altshuler of Columbia Records has a collection of two hundred thousand. But my collection is big enough to force me to move out of Paris—twenty miles north, into a house in a village. I have also practically every *Down Beat* that has come out since the first one in 1934. And I have pre-Civil War Spanish jazz magazines, and magazines from Japan and Uruguay and Chile. I have record catalogues from France and England and America between 1920 and 1940. I have more than a thousand books on jazz. The earliest, 'Le Jazz,' came out in 1926 and had one hundred and fifty-two pages. The first half was about African musical instruments, and the second half was about Paul Whiteman and George Gershwin. No jazz musician was mentioned in the book."

On Hugues Panassié: "Panassié was born on February 26, 1912. He was from a wealthy family. His father was in industry, but he died early. In his teens, Panassié was crippled by polio in one leg. Because he was crippled and because he was always educated by women, he became very spoiled as a child. I met him in Paris in 1934. He was living in the South of France. He had the gift to communicate his enthusiasm for the music to the people he talked to. That influenced me in a certain way, by helping me to understand things in the music that I didn't understand yet. He discovered more things in jazz than anyone before. He was right in the middle in 'Le Jazz Hot,' and he could see everything accurately. But in 1946, when a friend sent the first Dizzy Gillespie-Charlie Parker records to me in Paris, Panassié was in the South of France. Before he heard the records, I wrote about them in a Swiss magazine and André Hodeir wrote about them in *Hot Revue*, and Panassié, who was used to being the first, to being worshipped, would never accept Gillespie or Parker after that. The trouble is, when you get wrong, as Panassié was, and you want to defend your position, you're getting worse and worse. So since 1946 we never spoke again."

Stéphane Grappelli sees Panassié this way: "He was very sincere himself. He was a very pure man, very religious, very decent. Not for the gallery. He believed. He did a lot for the jazz music. The only bad thing about Panassié was he was a bit stubborn."

Ferdinand La Menthe*

Jelly Roll Morton, though long celebrated by jazz admirers, has yet to find his rightful place. (The Morton jazz industry has been going almost steadily since 1938, when Morton, threadbare and down on his luck, sat at a piano in the Library of Congress with the folklorist Alan Lomax and talked, sang, and played his life into a recording machine. Lomax later culled an autobiography, "Mister Jelly Roll," from the Library of Congress recordings, and selections from them have been issued on L.P.s from time to time.) Morton properly belongs in the nineteenth-century American mythology

* Long thought to be Jelly Roll Morton's real name. Now, according to recent research by Professor Larry Gushee of the University of Illinois, it seems that Morton was born Ferdinand Lamothe (the name of whites originally from Santo Domingo), and that he changed Lamothe to Mouton, which was finally corrupted to Morton. Gushee has also discovered that Morton was born in 1890, instead of 1885, and that his euphonious godmother Eulalie Echo was Laura Hécaud. Further, that Anita Gonzalez, his consort on the West Coast, was Bessie Johnson, a sister of the New Orleans musicians Bill, Dink, and Robert Johnson.

of Paul Bunyan and Johnny Appleseed and Davy Crockett, of the Yankee Peddlers and tall-tale tellers, of the circuses and minstrel shows. He made hustling his life's work. He was a pool player, a pimp, a bellhop, a tailor, a peddler, a cardsharp, a minstrel, a night-club manager, a fight promoter, and, when he had the time, a musician. He was a nomad, who lived or worked in New Orleans, where he was born, around 1885, and in Meridian, Jacksonville, St. Louis, Kansas City, Chicago, San Francisco, Detroit, Los Angeles, Memphis, Vancouver, Casper, Denver, Las Vegas, Tijuana, South Bend, Seattle, Davenport, Houston, Pittsburgh, Baltimore, Washington, D.C., and New York. He was outsize because of his variety and his ubiquity, and because he was a champion braggart. Morton bragged so much that his bragging took on an autonomous quality. He was already blowing his bugle in 1917, when he worked at the Cadillac Café in Los Angeles with Ada Smith, later known as the cabaret owner Bricktop. "His biggest conversation was always himself," she has said. "He'd run you out of your mind talking about himself. And he wasn't kidding. He meant it. He was always very temperamental, very hard to get along with. But Jelly was a genius before his time." Seven or eight years later, Alberta Hunter sang with him at the Pekin Café in Chicago, and she regards him somewhat differently: "He was a braggadocio and very good-natured." Morton told Lomax how, in his pre-Los Angeles days, he would disarm the female population when he landed in a small Southern town:

> I would . . . get a room, slick up, and walk down the street in my conservative stripe. The gals would all notice a new sport was in town, but I wouldn't so much as nod at anybody. Two hours later, I'd stroll back to my place, change into a nice tweed and stroll down the same way. The gals would begin to say, "My, my, who's this new flash-sport drop in town? He's mighty cute."
> About four in the afternoon, I'd come by the same way in an altogether different outfit and some babe would say, "Lawd, mister, how many suits you got anyway?"

I'd tell her, "Several, darling, several."

"Well, do you change like that every day?"

"Listen, baby, I can change like this every day for a month and never get my regular wardrobe half used up. I'm the suit man from suit land."

The next thing I know, I'd be eating supper in that gal's house and have a swell spot for meeting the sports, making my come-on with the piano and taking their money in the pool hall.

Morton claimed that he invented wire brushes, adapted "Tiger Rag" from a French quadrille and named it, started using the word "jazz," originated scat singing, and first used the washboard and the string bass on a recording. He claimed that "The Pearls" and "The Fingerbreaker," which he wrote, were the two most difficult jazz piano pieces of all time. But he floated his biggest balloon in 1938 when, piqued by a Robert Ripley "Believe It or Not" radio show in which W. C. Handy was described as the inventor of jazz and the blues, he sent an immense letter to the Baltimore *Afro-American* and to the magazine *down beat*. Here are parts:

It is evidently known, beyond contradiction, that New Orleans is the cradle of *jazz*, and I, myself, happened to be the creator in the year 1902.

I decided to travel, and tried Mississippi, Alabama, Florida, Tennessee, Kentucky, Illinois, and many other states during 1903-04, and was accepted as sensational.

I may be the only perfect specimen today in *jazz* that's living.

Speaking of jazz music, anytime it is mentioned musicians usually hate to give credit but they will say, "I heard Jelly Roll play it first."

Morton should have been genteel and reserved, for he was a Creole—a black Creole, or "Creole of color." In their great days in the nineteenth century, Creoles considered themselves the only genuine aristocracy in America. Morton was born Ferdinand La Menthe, and changed his name to Morton because, as he told Lomax, he "didn't want to be called Frenchy." His father, a carpenter and sometime trombonist named F. P. (Ed) La Menthe, soon vanished, and his mother, a light-skinned Creole named Louise Monette, died when he was fourteen. He apparently had little schooling, and he became a musician early. He tried the harmonica, the Jew's harp, the drums, the violin, the trombone, and the guitar before he settled on the piano—having cleared his head of the popular New Orleans belief that only sissies played the piano. He studied classical piano, and he learned from Tony Jackson, who wrote the song "Pretty Baby" and who appears to have been one of the few musicians whom Morton ungrudgingly admired. Jackson was "the greatest single-handed entertainer in the world," Morton told Lomax. "His memory seemed like something nobody's ever heard of in the music world. He was known as the man of a thousand songs. There was no tune that come up from any opera or any show of any kind or anything that was wrote on paper that Tony couldn't play. He had such a beautiful voice and a marvellous range." After Morton's mother died, he was left in the hands of an uncle and a great-grandmother, Mimi Pechet, but he was ostracized at fifteen by his great-grandmother when she discovered he had become a musician. (This snub may be one reason that Morton spent the rest of his life justifying himself, but it never deflected his loyalty to his family. Broke or not, he invariably sent money home.) Morton took off for Biloxi, where his godmother, Eulalie Echo, had a summer place, and he didn't settle down again for any length of time until he landed in Chicago twenty-odd years later. In Biloxi, he played piano in a whorehouse, started carrying a pistol, and had his first taste of whiskey, which didn't agree with him. (Booze may have gained on him as he grew older, for he pauses now and then on the Library of Congress records to say, "This whiskey is lovely.") Back in New Orleans, he played at Hilma Burt's whorehouse in Storyville. He took off down the Gulf Coast again and, turning up through Mississippi, was mistakenly arrested for having robbed a mail train. He was sentenced to a hundred days on the chain gang but escaped. He told Lomax that "it was some terrible environments that I went through in those days, inhabited by some very tough babies." In 1905, he returned to New Orleans, where he got in a fight in Pete Lala's saloon with Chicken Dick: "I hauled off and hit him with a pool ball and he jumped like he was made of rubber." Morton's sinning always had a testing, adolescent air; beyond a diamond or two, it never did him much good, and he never seems to have harmed anyone. He played more piano in Storyville, and he started writing music. At Tony Jackson's behest, he went to Chicago, where nothing was happening, and he then went down to Houston, where there were "only Jew's harps, harmonicas, mandolins, guitars, and fellows singing the spasmodic blues—sing awhile and pick awhile till they thought of another word to say." He paid his first visit to California, returned to New Orleans for the last time, and took off through the middle South with one Jack the Bear, selling Coca-Cola laced with salt as a cure for tuberculosis. He met W. C. Handy in Memphis in 1908, and three years later passed through New York, where he was heard by James P. Johnson. He joined several minstrel shows, was stranded in Hot Springs and St. Louis, turned up in Chicago again, and in 1917 landed in Los Angeles. He took up with Anita Gonzalez, a clever Creole he had known in New Orleans. They ran hotels and night clubs, and she may have bought him the famous diamond that moved back and forth the rest of his life between pawnshops and one of his front teeth. He turned up in Denver, where he played for the bandleader George Morrison, who was responsible for first bringing Paul Whiteman to New York. Morrison told Gunther Schuller, "He couldn't stay in one band too long, because he was too eccentric and too temperamental, and he was a one-man band himself . . . Oh, but he could stomp the blues out. When he got to pattin' that foot, playing the piano and a cigar in his mouth, man, he was gone—he was gone—he was gone!"

Morton lived in Chicago from 1923 to 1928, and it was the best part of his life. His reputation as a musician must have preceded him, for he made over thirty sides in his first year, including piano solos, duets and trios with King Oliver and with a clarinettist named Voltaire (Volly) de Faut, five numbers with the young white New Orleans Rhythm Kings, and almost a dozen numbers with bands of his own. He also worked his mouth. In the autobiography "Oh, Didn't He Ramble," the New Orleans trumpeter Lee Collins recalls that he and Morton ran around together. Morton "talked to me about making some records with him," Collins writes. "So one day I went over to see him [and] there he was—in bed with two women, one sitting on each side of him . . . Jelly wanted to know was I going to stay in Chicago or run on back home like a lot of other New Orleans musicians did. Then he asked me to come to work with him. 'You know that you will be working with the world's greatest jazz piano player.' . . . I told him I knew he was one of the greatest jazz pianists, but he said, 'Not one of the greatest— I am *the* greatest!' " Earl Hines remembers Morton, too. In "The World of Earl Hines," he told the critic Stanley Dance, "The three of them [the pianist Glover Compton, the dancer Lovey Taylor, and Morton] were the loudest fellows I ever heard. When they were standing on the corner, you could hear them for blocks. We used to go to ball games together, and you didn't have to know where they were sitting because you could hear them all over the White Sox park . . . If I came to the game late, I just followed their voices and found them." He also told Dance:

> Jelly Roll Morton . . . was the most popular underworld pianist around. [He] was a fair-complected man and sort of handsome. Nowadays you'd say he was overdressed, but he was the kind of fellow who carried his pearl-handled pistols with him and had plenty of money in his pocket at all times. If anybody tried to put him in a corner . . . he'd say things like, "I've got more suits than you've got handkerchiefs!" or, "I've been further around the world than you've been around a teacup!" He had written any number of tunes and everybody thought a lot of him. Whenever he needed money, he'd write a tune and sell it to one of the downtown

publishers like Melrose for fifty or seventy-five dollars. Tunes like "Milenberg Joys" were very popular, and when the bands began to play them he made a lot of money.

Morton may have made some money, but the Melrose brothers made a lot more, having also taken over Morton's "Jelly Roll Blues" (which was famous enough in 1917 to be mentioned in the lyrics of "The Darktown Strutters' Ball"), "The Wolverine Blues," and "King Porter Stomp," an anthem of the big-band era. (When Morton was sounding off years later in a Harlem club, an exasperated listener turned up a radio to drown him out, and "King Porter Stomp" came blasting out.) Late in 1926, the Melroses, intent on ballyhooing Morton's sheet music, got a recording contract for him with Victor, and during the next nine months he set down sixteen classic small-band sides under the name of Jelly Roll Morton and His Red Hot Peppers. He used two bands: George Mitchell on cornet, Omer Simeon or Johnny Dodds on clarinet, Kid Ory or George Bryant on trombone, Stump Evans on alto saxophone (six sides), Johnny St. Cyr or Bud Scott on banjo or guitar, John Lindsay on bass or Quinn Wilson on tuba, and Andrew Hilaire or Baby Dodds on drums. Morton had spent the previous twenty-five years as a hustler who also played the piano and led bands, and it has never been entirely clear where the originality, drive, lyric beauty, and rococo flair of these recordings came from. There is nothing as good anywhere else in Morton's musical life, nor is there anything quite like them anywhere in jazz. Roughness and delicacy, lyricism and straightforwardness, tension and relaxation, simplicity and complexity, campy humor and high seriousness, melody and improvisation, ensemble and solos—all are kept in an easy balance. Morton wrote the tunes (most of them a unique combination of ragtime and the blues), arranged them elaborately, and taught his musicians how to play them. Baby Dodds told Larry Gara, in "The Baby Dodds Story," what Morton did in a recording studio:

> At rehearsal Jelly Roll Morton used to work on each and every number until it satisfied him. Everybody had to

do just what Jelly wanted him to do . . . We used his
original numbers and he always explained what it was all
about and played a synopsis of it on the piano. Sometimes
we had music and he would mark with a pencil those places
which he wanted to stand out in a number. It was different
from recording with Louis [Armstrong]. Jelly didn't leave
much leeway for the individual musician . . . His own
playing was remarkable and kept us in good spirits. He
wasn't fussy, but he was positive . . . I never saw him upset and he didn't raise his voice at any time.

Morton's arrangements prefigured Duke Ellington's. He
used organ chords behind soloists and counterbalancing fragments of melody and riffs. He used a lot of breaks. He experimented with rhythmic devices and with the makeup of
his rhythm section. And he ceaselessly changed his instrumental combinations—a clarinet solo backed only by guitar,
and an a-cappella piano solo, a guitar solo backed by organ
chords—which gave the effect of a larger, more varied group.
He often wrote out the reed solos and the connective ensemble passages, but the main ensembles were jammed and
are perhaps the best instances we have of New Orleans poly-
phonic playing. The sixteen Victor sides range from the
stark to the baroque. "Jungle Blues" is deceptively simple.
It is based on a blueslike twelve-bar figure, set over a medium-tempo, two-note, rock-rock ostinato bass that persists
until the last two choruses. An ad-lib four-bar unison ensemble serves as an introduction, and in the first chorus the
cornet plays a melody over the ostinato bass, which is done
by the trombone and piano. Morton has Baby Dodds hit a
sour-sounding Chinese cymbal every four bars or so through
much of the record. The alto saxophone repeats the melody
in the second chorus, and a different melody, descending
and lyrical, is played by the ensemble for a chorus. Johnny
Dodds repeats this melody for a chorus, and there is another
ensemble stretch, accented by Baby Dodds' weird cymbal.
Morton comes out in a clearing with an unaccompanied
piano solo, but he carries on the ostinato bass in his left
hand, and near the close of the chorus he exchanges delicate
two-bar bits of melody with the guitar. The ostinato bass

stops, and the tuba, trombone, trumpet, and reeds play connected ascending two-bar breaks; then there is a fine closing
two-chorus ensemble and a four-bar coda that echoes the
introduction. Morton establishes a monochromatic, metro-
nomic air in the first chorus and spends the rest of the record slowly breaking it down with affecting melodic breezes,
loose, ambling ensembles, and the lyrical, summer-evening
exchanges between him and the guitar.

Morton's bands were his sounding boards. There are no
stray hairs or ragged cuffs on the 1926-27 sides. Everything
fits and flows, and there is never any loss of spontaneity or
swing. Each side is multilayered but clear, highly tinted but
not gaudy, tailored but not stiff. The records are a distilla-
tion of what Morton heard around him in New Orleans during the first decade of the century. They combine with
great ease absolute opposites: ragtime, a complex written
music that depends on the fluency of its performers and the
grace of its melodies for the rather thin emotional responses
it provokes; and the blues, a loose harmonic progression,
often clothed with notes that don't exist (the so-called blue
notes), and mysteriously capable of evoking almost every
kind of emotion.

Not long after Morton had recorded the last of the Chicago
Red Hot Pepper sides, he moved to New York, which was
rapidly becoming the center of the music. One of jazz's
lightning shifts in musical emphasis had preceded him, and
when he arrived he found he had gone out of fashion. His
music was basically an ensemble music, an arranger's music,
and jazz had suddenly become a music of soloists—Louis
Armstrong, Coleman Hawkins, Jimmy Harrison, Jabbo
Smith, Benny Goodman. Nonetheless, Morton made more
sides for Victor between 1928 and 1930, when his contract
ran out, than he had made in five years in Chicago. Some are
minor classics—"Georgia Swing," "Kansas City Stomps,"
"Boogaboo," "Shoe Shiners Drag," "Shreveport Stomp,"
"Mournful Serenade," "Deep Creek," "Tank Town Bump,"

"Smilin' the Blues Away," and "Turtle Twist"—but none quite match the freshness and originality of the Chicago recordings. Morton had an infallible ear for talent, and the young musicians on his New York recordings who became well known include Red Allen, J. C. Higginbotham, Cozy Cole, Russell Procope, Walter Foots Thomas, Sandy Williams, and Tommy Benford. When he wasn't recording, he scrambled. He fronted bands briefly at the Rose Danceland, the Checker Club, and the Lido Ballroom. He put together a revue, "Speeding Along," and worked in Laura Prampin's band in Coney Island. He took pickup groups to country clubs around New York for Saturday-night dances, and he took bands on the road in Pennsylvania and Ohio and New England. He played solo piano at the Red Apple Club, at Seventh Avenue and 135th Street. In photographs of him taken in the thirties in Harlem, he seems always to be talking and gesticulating and smiling. He was a striking-looking man, with a long, aquiline nose, a strong chin, and a high forehead. (Alberta Hunter found him "tall and ugly, with the longest fingers I ever saw.") A number of people who knew him are still around, and here are some of their voices. The first is the guitarist Lawrence Lucie:

> Jelly was a walking encyclopedia, and he was very entertaining. He always smiled after he said something outrageous. He knew exactly what he wanted in his music, and he believed in his style. Some people thought he was old-fashioned, but he was greater than we all thought he was. He'd been ahead of his time for a long time before times caught up to him.

Walter Foots Thomas (reeds):

> Jelly sent for me in Indiana. I was afraid to come to New York. I could read, but I didn't play too much jazz. Jelly influenced my style and my musical thinking, and he inspired me to write. I used to watch him sit down and write a piece off, just like that. He wrote a lot of the clarinet solos in his arrangements, but he didn't write the brass solos. I always felt that his melodies came from New Orleans

but that his rhythms came from the Latin countries. When he went on a tour of colleges in Pennsylvania, I drove the band bus. He used to talk all the time about "that good Gulf gas," how he couldn't live without "that good Gulf gas."

Doc Cheatham (trumpet):

Jelly was a born player, he just naturally stomped. In Chicago, he knew he was the king. He had gold coins in the tips of his shoes, and he wore diamond rings. But he was in bad shape in New York. I think I was one of the few friends he had. He liked me, and when I played he'd say, "Damn! That's the way to play the trumpet. These somebodies don't know *nothing!*"

Bernard Addison (guitar):

Jelly was fine people. He talked aplenty, but I presume he knew what he was talking about. I used to hear him bragging on street corners in Harlem, and he used to hold audiences at the Rhythm Club, where there would be ten or twenty musicians around him. I only made recording dates with him. We rehearsed an hour or so, and then went on wax. Most of what we recorded was by head. I don't think he was in the capacity of Willie the Lion Smith or James P. Johnson. He was more in the honky-tonk style.

Morton was a very different pianist from Smith or Johnson or Fats Waller. He used the stride bass sparingly, and his right hand was less lacy and staccato. He used tenths in his left hand, boogie-woogie bases, offbeat chords, single notes, and silences. His right-hand figures were often more daring than those of the Harlem stride pianists. He liked advanced chords, and he liked to double or triple the time, or slow it down, or use arrhythmic figures. Unlike the stride pianists, he was a good blues player. Stanley Dance thinks that Morton had more influence on Earl Hines in the twenties than is generally acknowledged, and he is probably right. Morton is visible in Hines' accompanying, in his arrhythmic bursts, and in his over-all legato attack. Mary Lou

Williams has long admitted that Morton was her first model. More voices. The first is the recording executive Ahmet Ertegun:

My brother Nesuhi and I used to drive up to New York from Washington for the Sunday-afternoon jam sessions. It must have been 1939 or 1940. Jelly Roll appeared for a short while in a band led by Sidney Bechet. Big Sid Catlett was there, and Sidney de Paris and Albert Nicholas and Claude Jones, and possibly Omer Simeon. Jelly talked a lot between numbers—about how he invented jazz and that sort of thing. He always looked dapper and had style. If anybody invented jazz, he did, because he predicted so much that was to come. The greatest jazz record of all time is "Shreveport Stomp," with Simeon and Tommy Benford. It was bright and brassy and seven years ahead of the Benny Goodman trio. Obviously, Jelly was the greatest person in jazz—with all due respect to Louis and Duke.

Nesuhi Ertegun (recording executive):

Kid Ory told me about a record session Morton had in Chicago in 1923 on the old Okeh label. Zue Robertson was on trombone, and he refused to play the melody of one of the tunes the way Morton wanted it played. Jelly took a big pistol out of his pocket and put it on the piano, and Robertson played the melody note for note.

John Hammond (recording executive, critic):

I used to see Jelly around New York during the depths of the Depression, around 1934 or 1935, and he was seedy and disillusioned. He sang and played at a place on Seventh Avenue called the Red Apple. Lester Young used to drop in there after Basie came to town. In 1934, I did a Wingy Manone date for Vocalion, and Wingy insisted on bringing Jelly Roll in. He was sloppy that day, and nobody on the date felt good about him. Somewhere around that time, I read that Duke Ellington was to appear at a theatre in Queens, and I went out, but who should turn up but Jelly Roll and a non-union band that included the trombonist Charlie Irvis. I don't think there were sixty people in the whole place.

Willie, the Lion Smith had little tolerance for fools, and in his "Music on My Mind" he wrote, "Morton was a man with strong spiritual and magnetic forces; when he sat down to play he could hold an audience by the strength of his strong personality. He was a sharpshooter and had always travelled in fast company. He was intelligent, had something to offer, and as far as I could tell, he was always able to back up what he said." When Alan Lomax was doing his book on Morton, he went to see Mabel Bertrand, a dancer whom Morton had married just before coming to New York. She talked of Morton's fastidiousness:

> He was very particular . . . When he'd taken a shirt off, he would miss it if I didn't launder it that day . . . He would go through the drawer, looking for that particular shirt.
>
> I'd say to him, "What you looking for?"
>
> "I'm looking for that pink-striped shirt."
>
> "It must be in the chiffonier," I'd say, but he'd go straight to the bathroom, find it in the clothes basket. "Is it getting too hard for you to do the laundry?" Jelly would say.
>
> "No."
>
> "May, I'm trying to make it easy on you. Isn't it easier to wash and iron *one* shirt just when I take it off than to wait and let them pile up?"
>
> "Yes."
>
> "You don't have a thing in the world to do but keep my laundry clean."

Morton got a little crazy in the mid-thirities. He lost money in a business venture, and he became convinced that a voodoo spell had been put on him. In 1935, he moved to Washington, D.C., and ended up in a little second-floor club in the black district. The photographer William P. Gottlieb remembers him there: "It had a piano and a few chairs, and Morton would tend bar and seat people and sometimes play piano. It was a pretty bare place, and I never saw more than a handful of people. Jelly had a big hole in the front tooth where he'd had his diamond, and his face got all crinkled when he smiled. He had a routine he used to

go through about how he needed such-and-such a break to
reëstablish himself. He had plenty of bravado, and he exuded
optimism. It was a front he never let down." Lomax recorded Morton in the spring of 1938, and Morton wrote his
famous letter to the papers. People suddenly remembered
that he was alive, and in 1939 he was asked to record eight
sides for Bluebird with such as Sidney Bechet, Sidney de
Paris, Zutty Singleton, Lawrence Lucie, Claude Jones, and
Albert Nicholas. During December, 1939, and January, 1940,
he made his last records—a dozen or so piano solos and a
dozen band sides. The band sides are dumpy and shrill, but
the piano sides, particularly those with Morton vocals, are
splendid. He was a beautiful singer, with a gentle baritone
voice and marvellous phrasing—one of the best of all jazz
singers—and it's a pity he didn't sing more. In the fall of
1940, he heard that Eulalie Echo, his godmother, had died
in California, and, fearing that some diamonds she had would
be stolen, he decided to head West. He still owned two big
old cars, and he hooked them together and set off by himself. On November 9th, he wrote to Mabel Bertrand from
Yreka, California, telling her, in fine Morton fashion, that
he had hit snowstorms in ten states, that he had slid off the
road in Wyoming, that he had had to abandon one car in
Montpelier, Idaho, and that he had got stuck on a mountain
in Oregon and had to be rescued by the police. The diamonds were gone, but he stayed on. David Stuart, who now
owns an art gallery in Los Angeles, got to know Morton:

> I had my Jazz Man Record Shop, and Jelly used to come
> in, and we became friendly. He loved to talk about the
> past, and he had a terrific memory. He said that he'd writ-
> ten fourteen hundred songs, that there had been a period
> in the twenties when he'd write a song a night. One after-
> noon, a friend and I were driving Jelly around with the
> thought of stopping to visit the trombonist Zue Robertson.
> Robertson had a sister in Los Angeles, and he lived in a
> kind of chicken coop behind her house, and he wanted
> nothing so much as to get back to New Orleans. Jelly
> figured out what we had in mind before we got there, and

he absolutely refused to go. "No, sir. He hates me, he hates me," he kept saying. Sometimes we'd take him out to hear music in the evening—Kid Ory and Mutt Carey, old New Orleans people like that. The musicians called him "The Roll," and when he appeared they'd all stand up and say, "Here comes the Roll." He got sick before he died, and they put him in a kind of broom closet in the hospital, and they treated him shabbily. I'd go over in the afternoon and sit with him. He'd hold my hand hour after hour, even though I'm sure he had no idea who I was anymore.

Morton died July 10, 1941. The Ellington and Lunceford bands, both in their prime, were playing in Los Angeles, but no one from either group went to the funeral.

Le Grand Bechet

The great New Orleans clarinettist and soprano saxophonist
Sidney Bechet was, like Morton, a Creole of color. He was
born in 1897, the youngest of seven children. His father,
Omar, was a cornettist and a shoemaker, and his mother,
Josephine, was an octoroon who loved to dance. When he
was six, he was playing the clarinet and taking lessons from
the New Orleans master George Baquet, and soon afterward
he went to work in his brother Leonard's band. When he
was sixteen or seventeen, he and Clarence Williams (the
pianist and composer) rode the rods into Texas. Bechet got
into a fight with a white man, and fled to Galveston, where
another brother lived. At twenty, he joined the Bruce &
Bruce Stock Company, and ended up in Chicago. He had
played with everyone of consequence in New Orleans (Bunk
Johnson, Buddy Petit, King Oliver, Louis Armstrong), and
in Chicago he played with Lil Hardin and Roy Palmer, and
then with the cornettist Freddie Keppard—another icono-
clast, whom he admired enormously. He was heard by the

bandleader Will Marion Cook, who had a large, Paul White-
man-type ensemble, and Cook hired him as a soloist (Bechet
could not read music, and never fully learned) and took him
to England. It was June of 1919, and Bechet was a sensation.
Ernest Ansermet, a thirty-five-year-old Swiss who had conducted the première of Stravinsky's "L'Histoire du Soldat,"
went repeatedly to hear the band. He also talked with
Bechet, and in due course wrote a review in the Swiss *Revue
Romande.* Here is part of the last, prescient paragraph:

> There is in the Southern Syncopated Orchestra an ex-
> traordinary clarinet virtuoso who is, so it seems, the first of
> his race to have composed perfectly formed blues on the
> clarinet. I've heard two of them which he had elaborated at
> great length [and] they are equally admirable for their
> richness of invention, force of accent, and daring in novelty
> and the unexpected. Already, they gave the idea of a style,
> and their form was gripping, abrupt, harsh, with a brusque
> and pitiless ending like that of Bach's second "Brandenburg
> Concerto." I wish to set down the name of this artist of
> genius; as for myself, I shall never forget it—it is Sidney
> Bechet. . . . What a moving thing it is to meet this very
> black, fat boy with white teeth and that narrow forehead,
> who is very glad one likes what he does, but who can say
> nothing of his art, save that he follows his "own way" . . .
> His "own way" is perhaps the highway the whole world
> will swing along tomorrow.

Cook disbanded, and Bechet stayed on with a drummer
named Benny Peyton. Then Bechet got into hot water over
an English prostitute and was deported, despite his having
bewitched the Royal Family at a command performance at
Buckingham Palace. Back in America, he went into a show
called "How Come?," with Bessie Smith. Bechet liked Bessie
Smith. This is how he described her in "Treat It Gentle,"
his autobiography: "She could be plenty tough . . . She always drank plenty and she could hold it, but sometimes,
after she'd been drinking a while, she'd get like there was
no pleasing her. There were times you had to know just
how to handle her right." He played with James P. Johnson

at the Kentucky Club, and around 1924 joined the fledgling
Duke Ellington band. Ellington never got over Bechet's
great lyrical bent. He wrote of him in "Music Is My Mistress":

> Often, when Bechet was blowing, he would say, "I'm
> going to call Goola this time!" Goola was his dog, a big
> German shepherd. Goola wasn't always there, but he was
> calling him anyway with a kind of throaty growl.
> *Call* was very important in that kind of music. Today,
> the music has grown up and become quite scholastic, but
> this was *au naturel,* close to the primitive, where people
> send messages in what they play, calling somebody, or mak-
> ing facts and emotions known. Painting a picture, or having
> a story to go with what you were going to play, was of
> vital importance in those days. The audience didn't know
> anything about it, but the cats in the band did.

Bechet slipped away from Ellington, and opened a place of
his own, the Club Basha. Then, never still long, he returned
to Europe, with Claude Hopkins and Josephine Baker, for a
show called "Revue Nègre." Bechet put down his European
roots during the twenties. He toured Russia, and roamed
Western Europe. But he got into another fracas, in 1928.
One morning around eight, he and the American banjoist
Little Mike McKendrick had a gun battle outside a Mont-
martre bar. Bechet grazed McKendrick, hit the pianist
Glover Compton in the leg, and wounded a Frenchwoman
on her way to work. He went to jail for eleven months.
When he got out, he worked at the Wild West Bar in Berlin
and then went back to New York. In 1932, he joined Duke
Ellington again, and tutored Johnny Hodges on the soprano
saxophone, thus indirectly and permanently altering the Ellington band. Bechet put together the first of his New Orleans Feetwarmers bands and took it into the Savoy Ballroom, in Harlem. The group, which included the trumpeter
Tommy Ladnier and the pianist Hank Duncan, made six
numbers for Victor, which are among the most joyous and
swinging of all jazz records. Bechet had met Ladnier in Russia, and the two men spent much time together in the thir-

ties. When the Depression closed in, they quit the music and started a sort of basement store in Harlem, called the Southern Tailor Shop. The pianist Willie the Lion Smith remembered it in "Music on My Mind":

> I'd ask Sidney where he was living.
> He would reply, "I'm at 129th Street and St. Nicholas. I'm the proprietor of the Southern Tailor Shop."
> That would gas me. I couldn't figure out what a good jazz clarinet player was doing playing "tailor."
> So I said, "How many suits you got in there?"
> "Oh," he said, "I've got up to about twenty; but we don't make them, just press 'em."
> Then I asked, "Who's we?"
> He replied, "Tommy and myself."
> Well, I knew Tommy Ladnier from Chicago days. He was a good trumpet player. I found out later that Sidney would press and repair the suits, while Ladnier specialized in shining shoes. . . .
> Bechet mentioned they had some good sessions in the back of the shop. So one night I agreed to come around to see what was happening.
> But first, I wanted some information. "How much you charge to press a suit?"
> He replied, "Oh, the regular fee."
> You see I figured if nothing was going on I could at least get my suit pressed. Then I wanted to know, "What do we sleep on?"
> He then said, "I've got a couple of cots in the back. But usually there's a bunch of musicianers playing back there."
> "You ain't gonna press any clothes tonight then," I said.
> "No, man. I cooked up a batch of red beans and rice to add to a lot of cold fried chicken. We'll have us a party."

When the drummer Zutty Singleton arrived in New York from Chicago in 1937, he moved into the building Bechet and Ladnier shared quarters in. Singleton once said, "They called their place the House of Meditation, and they had a picture of Beethoven on the wall. One day, Ladnier said to Bechet, 'You know something, Bash? You the dead image of Beethoven,' and that pleased Bechet. Bechet and Ladnier would stand in front of this big old mirror they had and watch themselves while they practiced. They listened to classical music, and they talked a lot about their travels— when Bechet wasn't talking about the Rosicrucians. He was a hell of a cat. He could be mean. He could be sweet. He could be in between."

Jazz concerts were beginning to take hold by 1940, and that year Bechet gave one in Washington, D.C. It was organized by the recording executive Nesuhi Ertegun. "Not long after I came to the United States, I decided to give a jazz concert built around Sidney Bechet," Ertegun has said. "My father was the Turkish Ambassador, and I lived at the Embassy in Washington, so I decided to give it in Washington. I had in mind a concert with a mixed band and a mixed audience, but Washington was still a Southern racist town, and no concert hall would touch such an affair. Finally, the Jewish Community Center, which had a four-hundred-seat auditorium, agreed. In addition to Bechet, I wanted Sidney De Paris on trumpet, Vic Dickenson on trombone, Art Hodes on piano, Wellman Braud on bass, and Manzie Johnson on drums. The alternating group would be Meade Lux Lewis and the blues shouter Joe Turner. I found Bechet at the Mimmo Club, in Harlem. He was backing a slick show, with a chorus line and singers and all that, and the band was in tuxedos. It all looked very prosperous. But the truth was that Bechet, who was already a hero in France, wasn't doing at all well here. The next day, he invited me to his apartment for a drink and something to eat. After we sat down, his wife came in and said to Bechet, 'Who's that? What does he want?' Bechet introduced me and said he'd brought me home for a bite. She said, 'You know there's no food in this house. Now, go on, get out and find your own food!' We went to a bar and had a drink and worked out the details of the concert. When the band arrived in Washington, they came to the Embassy, and we had an elegant lunch. I knew Bechet loved red beans and rice, so we had red beans and rice, and he was astonished. He wanted to know if we had a Creole cook, and I said no, a Turkish cook, and that beans and rice was a common dish in Turkey, too. Bechet couldn't believe it, and he said we must be copying the Creoles, and a very pleasant argument went on for some time about the roots of red beans and rice. The musicians were relaxed and in a good mood, and the concert, which was in the afternoon, was a tremendous success musically.

"From then on, Sidney and I were very friendly. He was deceptive. With his white hair and round face, he looked much older than he was. He also had this genial, sweet Creole politeness and a beautiful, harmonious way of talking. In many ways, he seemed like a typical Uncle Tom. But once you got to know him—once you had broken the mirror and got inside and found the true Bechet—you discovered he wasn't that way at all. He couldn't stand fakery or hypocrisy, and he was a tough and involved human being. He was far more intelligent than people took him for, and he knew what was going on everywhere. I never heard him play badly, even with bad groups. He was an incredibly rich player. Years later, when I was running a John Coltrane record date, Coltrane told me that Bechet had been an important influence on him."

Like most New Orleans clarinettists, Bechet used the Albert-system clarinet, which has a formal, luxurious, Old World tone. New Orleans clarinet playing tended to be rich and florid. Vibratos were wide, glissandi were favored, and emotions were high and unashamed. Bechet, along with Johnny Dodds, Jimmy Noone, and Barney Bigard, belonged to the second generation of New Orleans clarinettists. (The first included Alphonse Picou, Lorenzo Tio, Jr., Big Eye Louis Nelson, and George Baquet.) Noone and Bigard concentrated on legato attacks, fed and enriched their tones, and perfected showy melodic swoops and arcs. They liked being serene and airborne. Bechet and Dodds were rhythm players. They broke up their phrases ingeniously, used a great many blue notes, and had acidic, almost disagreeable timbres. Bechet used growls, strange bubbling sounds, and wide, swaggering notes. He shook his sounds out. When he took up the soprano saxophone, in the early twenties, he transferred his clarinet playing to this odd and difficult instrument. The soprano saxophone defies being played on pitch, and Bechet and his star pupil, Bob Wilber, are practically its only pitch-perfect practitioners. (The deliberate tonal distortions used by many modern soprano saxophonists make it impossible to tell whether they are in tune.) Bechet developed an enormous tone that incorporated qualities of the trumpet, the oboe, and the horn. The sheer strength of his sound, and his rhythmic drive, allowed him to rule every band he played in. Wise trumpet players stood aside or were blown to smithereens. As an improviser, Bechet used the chords of a song but also followed the melody, which kept reappearing, like sunlight on a forest floor. His melodic lines were pronouncements. They were full of shouts and swoops; they gleamed and exploded. The solos left his listeners with the feeling that they had been in on important things. When he played a slow blues, he exhibited a melancholy, an ancient grieving. And when he played a slow ballad he was honeyed and insinuating and melodramatic. Johnny Hodges grew up in both sides of this divided house.

In 1946, Bechet moved to Brooklyn and opened a sort of music school. The jazz critic Richard Hadlock took some lessons from him, and wrote about them in the San Francisco *Examiner:*

> Sidney would run off a complex series of phrases and leave me alone in his room for a couple of hours to wrestle with what he had played. One lesson could easily take up an entire afternoon, and Sidney favored giving a lesson every day.
>
> "Look, when you emphasize a note, you throw your whole body into it," he would say, cutting a wide arc with his horn as he slashed into a phrase.
>
> "I'm going to give you one note today," he once told me. "See how many ways you can play that note—growl it, smear it, flat it, sharp it, do anything you want to it. That's

how you express your feelings in this music. It's like talking.
"Always try to complete your phrases and your ideas . . .
There are lots of otherwise good musicians who sound terrible because they start a new idea without finishing the
last one."

Bob Wilber has described another facet of Bechet:

One thing he was very interested in was the concept of
interpreting a song. You start out with an exposition of the
melody in which you want to bring out the beauty of it. And
then you start your variations, but at first they are closely
related to the melody. Then, as you go on to another chorus,
you get further away—you do something a little less based
on the melody but more on the harmony. Sidney was much
more harmonically oriented than most of the players of his
generation . . . Then at the end, you would come back to
the melody and there would be some kind of coda which
would bring the thing to a conclusion. . . . The idea of the
form was very important to him.

Bechet settled in France in 1951. He had filled the forties
with gigs in and around New York and in Chicago. The
pianist Dick Wellstood worked with him at Jazz Limited, in
Chicago, and at the Bandbox, in New York. "He was very
autocratic and nineteenth-century," Wellstood once said.
"It was like working for Bismarck. There was a right way
and a wrong way, and if you did it the wrong way it was
mutiny. There was a right tempo and right chords, and
that was the way you reached the people. He had a gentlemanly and courtly exterior. He spoke softly, using the New
Orleans accent of 'poil' and 'erster' for 'pearl' and 'oyster.'
But when he was annoyed he'd lash out, and I think he always carried a knife. Once, at Jimmy Ryan's, in New York,
his piano player was late, and Bechet asked me—I just happened to be there—to sit in. When the piano player arrived,
Sidney bawled him out publicly, and told him, 'I want you
to give that boy five dollars.' I think he got increasingly
egocentric. At the Bandbox, he sat in a thronelike chair
backstage, and people paid court to him. Alfred Lion, of

Blue Note records, would bring him champagne and all but kneel at his feet. His sense of humor was strange. One night, in Chicago, he played this game with his trombonist Munn Ware. The horn players were supposed to stand up to solo, but after Sidney had taken his solo and sat down and Munn had stood up Sidney got up again and started playing and Munn sat down. Sidney played several choruses and sat down, and when Munn stood up again to solo Sidney stood up, and on it went. Later, Munn shot him in the back of the head with a water pistol, and I waited for lightning to strike, but Sidney only giggled. The truth is, I was scared to death of him the whole time I worked for him."

Bechet's autobiography, done in France with the help of Joan Reid, Desmond Flower, and John Ciardi, was published the year after his death, in 1959. The first two-thirds of the book is remarkable. It opens with a long, mythlike account of the life and death of his grandfather, a freed slave named Omar. Omar becomes obsessed with a young slave girl on a nearby plantation, and one night he takes her to the edge of the bayou and makes love to her. But the girl's owner, also bewitched by her, follows them. He shoots Omar in the arm and takes the girl home. Then he spreads word that Omar has raped his daughter and search parties scour the bayou, where Omar hides. He sees the girl once more, at great peril, and is murdered by a slave seeking the reward. The girl has a baby, who becomes Bechet's father. It does not matter how much improvisation there is in the story. Bechet's language is dense and mysterious and poetical:

> All those trees there, they was standing like skeletons after the hide of the animal has disappeared. There was moonlight on their tops like blossoming, and there was the darkness under them, the light and the darkness somehow part of one thing that was darker than just plain dark, and all so still.

The book is full of folk wisdom:

> So many people go at themselves like they was some book: they look back through themselves, they see this so and so chapter, they remember this one thing or another,

but they don't go through the pages one after the other really finding out what they're about and who they are and where they are. They never count their whole story together.

He talks of spirituals and the blues:

In the spirituals the people clapped their hands—that was their rhythm. In the blues it was further down; they didn't need the clapping, but they remembered it . . . And both of them, the spirituals and the blues, they was a prayer. One was praying to God and the other was praying to what's human. It's like one was saying, "Oh, God, let me go," and the other was saying, "Oh, Mister, let me be."

Bechet's life in France appears to have fulfilled him. He married a German woman he had known in the twenties, and he kept a mistress, by whom he had a son. He made a lot of money, bought a small estate outside Paris, and drove a Salmson coupé at high speeds. In 1957, he recorded a tight, to-the-point collaboration with the prickly modern French pianist Martial Solal. It is one of his best records. The next year, he played beautifully at the Brussels World's Fair. The impresario and pianist George Wein was in the band. "I never encountered the evil side of Bechet," Wein has said. "Two things that probably caused it were his stomach, which bothered him for years, and trumpet players who tried to grab the lead in bands he was in. I think he was kind to musicians who were his inferiors, and hard on musicians who were his equals. I filled in at a Bechet concert at the Academy of Music, in Philadelphia, in 1948, when James P. Johnson failed to show, and he *made* me feel like I was playing beautifully, even on 'Summertime,' which was his big number, and which I'd never played before. He was a great lyrical force, and he had great personal force. He filled a room when he came into it. I think he could have been as big as Louis Armstrong if he hadn't mistrusted all bookers and managers. There was no reason for Bechet to come back from France after he settled there. He was happy and was worshipped. But he did come back a few times in the early fifties, and on one of his visits he played a gig at Storyville, my club in Boston. His stomach acted up, and we put him in Massachusetts General Hospital. They told him he had to have an operation, and what did he do? He went back to France and had the operation there. He trusted the French more than he did the Americans. Until the very end, that is. I was in France in 1959, and Charles Delaunay told me that Sidney was dying. I called him up at his house outside Paris and asked him what I could do. 'Come and see me,' he said. I'm very bad at such visits, but I went, and Sidney told me he wanted to go home. I told him O.K., we'd try and make arrangements and such, but before anything could be done he was gone."

New York Drummers

For a long time, drummers held jazz together. They kept the beat, colored and shaded ensembles, lifted soloists, added timbres and textures, hypnotized audiences, and determined the very sound and character of a band. Consider the Woody Herman band with Dave Tough (1944–45) and the Woody Herman band with Don Lamond (1945–49), the Duke Ellington band with Sonny Greer (1920-51) and with Louis Bellson (1951-53), the Modern Jazz Quartet with Kenny Clarke (1952-55) and with Connie Kay (1955-74). Drummers reigned during the twenties and thirties and forties and into the fifties, when their function began slowly and subtly to change. Instead of keeping time—in much of the avantgarde, there is no longer any time to keep—they now assemble a surrealistic flow of cymbal, snare-drum, and tom-tom sounds, and they are frequently noted for their "melodic" attacks. The drummer's position has been seized by the bassist, who, armed with electricity and with guitar and sitar techniques, has become a rhythmic bully. In their great days, drummers congregated in New York, where they could sit in and show their wares, and where they could engage in "cutting" contests with other drummers. Some of those New York drummers are almost unknown, and some are world famous. Some spent decades in New York, and some only a few months: Tony Sbarbaro, Kaiser Marshall, Freddie Moore, George Stafford, Old Man Brooks, Tommy Benford, Baby Dodds, Zutty Singleton, Bill Beason, Sonny Greer, Keg Purnell, Slick Jones, Art Trappier, Cuba Austin, Manzie Johnson, Chick Webb, Walter Johnson, Arthur Herbert, Alphonse Steele, Ben Pollack, Sam Weiss, Joe Grauso, Chauncey Morehouse, Stan King, Vic Berton, Razz Mitchell, Alvin Burroughs, Yank Porter, Harry Dial, Cozy Cole, Paul Barbarin, Sid Catlett, Gene Krupa, Dave Tough, Jo Jones, Lionel Hampton, O'Neil Spencer, Jimmy Crawford, Cliff Leeman, Moe Purtill, Danny Alvin, George Wettling, Ray Bauduc, Ray McKinley, Nick Fatool, Buddy Rich, Louis Bellson, Lee Young, Specs Powell, Shelly Manne, J. C. Heard, Eddie Dougherty, Gus Johnson, Panama Francis, Kansas Fields, Jack the Bear Parker, Morey Feld, Kenny Clarke, Art Blakey, Denzil Best, Max Roach, Hal West, Osie Johnson, Shadow Wilson, Tiny Kahn, Roy Haynes, Art Taylor, Specs Wright, Philly Joe Jones, Sam Woodyard, Joe Morello, Charlie Persip, Sonny Igoe, Mousey Alexander, Don Lamond, Ed Shaughnessy, Connie Kay, Jimmy Madison, Mel Lewis, Jake Hanna.

Jazz drumming grew out of military drumming. The pioneer jazz drummers picked up syncopation from ragtime and translated it into afterbeats and offbeats and press rolls, most of them carried out on the snare drum and tomtoms. By the thirties, the center of jazz drumming had shifted to the cymbals and the snare-drum rims, although the snare and tomtoms were still heavily used in solos. The bebop drummers moved the center again. They transferred timekeeping from the bass drum to a "ride" cymbal, using the bass drum only for offbeats, or "bombs." In the twenties, drum sets, or traps (which were invented when drummers began to play sitting down), consisted of a tall, fat bass drum, often decorated with a painting of a bucolic scene and lit from within by an electric bulb, which also kept dampness at bay; a wooden-sided snare drum that resembled a parade drum; an Indian tomtom, its skins fastened on with brass studs; and a cymbal attached upside down to the wooden top of the bass drum. By the late twenties, the snare drum had become sensitive enough to be used with wire brushes—sprays of steel wire fastened to metal or wooden handles. There were several tomtoms and several cymbals, which were hung over the bass drum on goosenecked or straight rods. Two more cymbals, called a high-hat, appeared at the drummer's left elbow on a three-foot metal stand, and were opened and closed by a foot pedal to produce a marvellous variety of whispers, shushes, splashes, and whaps. Drummers had begun to pay attention to the sound of their instrument; they tuned their snare drums and tomtoms and bass drums, and they spent long reverberating hours selecting their cymbals at the Zildjian factory, in Quincy, Massachusetts. The bebop drummers did disturbing things to the drum set in the forties. Their snare drums grew thinner and thinner, and emitted a high nervous chatter; the bass drums shrank, and their sound grew sharp and peevish; and the cymbals became larger and larger, and gave out a heavy, high hum. The drum sets now used by many rock and "fusion" drummers are works of fantasy. The drums, which are frequently made of translucent plastic, seem to multiply before one's eyes, and may include a couple of bass drums and snare drums, and at least four tomtoms. A dozen giant, steeply canted cymbals form a reflecting shield around this assemblage, which is lit from below, so that it produces an aurora-borealis effect, with the drummer at its brilliant, frenzied center.

The older drummers have not vanished. Many are constantly busy, among them Buddy Rich and Freddie Moore and Art Blakey and Shelly Manne and Tommy Benford and Lionel Hampton and Roy Haynes and Sonny Greer. Three of them—by virtue of their tenure, their distinguished style, and their undiminished skill—should be celebrated. All

three are in their seventies. They are Benford, Moore, and
Greer.

Tommy Benford was born in Charleston, West Virginia, on
what he likes to call "the nineteenth day of the fourth
month of oh-five." He is short, neat, and forthright, and has
a gruff voice, flat gray hair, and a square bespectacled face.
There is a metallic cast to him; if he were struck with one
of his mallets, he would ring. He has never been famous,
but he was one of the first modern drummers. He taught
Chick Webb when Webb arrived in New York, in 1924, at
the age of twenty-two; and he and Sid Catlett traded inventions in the early thirties. Catlett went on to become the
supreme jazz drummer, and Benford became his indefatig-
able image. His accompanying recalls Catlett's. He uses
similar cymbal and bass-drum breaks, and some of the same
intricate snare-drum figures—holding one stick on the drum-
head and hitting it with the other, then letting the stationary
stick bounce once on the head, to produce a quick, echoing
eighth note. His rare solos are short, and are an even mixture
of rolls and rimshots and cymbals. His wire-brush work is
tricky and adroit. Benford sits very straight when he plays,
and his time is prim and exact. He is rarely in need of work,
and in recent years has appeared with Bob Greene's band,
which creates uncanny resurrections of Jelly Roll Morton's
music; with Dick Wellstood's Fats Waller bands at Michael's
Pub; with Bob Wilber and Kenny Davern's Soprano Summit; and with the Dick Hyman group that has backed
Twyla Tharp. Benford's memory hovers around him, and
when he needs an address or a name from fifty or more
years ago it is handed to him forthwith. He talks easily, and
he often surrounds his sentences with buffering silences,
which give his speech a beneficent, upholstered air. He is a
proud man, and he walks with his head slightly raised and
his arms stiff as drumsticks at his sides. Here is what he
said:
   "I went to Europe the first time in 1932 with Sy Dev-

ereaux, who had a seven-piece band. We opened at the Chez Florence, in Paris, and—oh, my God!—Europe was really Europe then. We couldn't do wrong. The pianos were *always* in tune and everything was always clean, and every club, no matter how small, had a room for the musicians to go to between sets—not like it is here, where you have to walk up and down the sidewalk when you're not playing. I worked with Freddie Taylor, who had his own club, the Chez Harlem, and then with Eddie South, who was billed as the 'dark angel' of the violin. I worked in Holland a lot, and at the Paris Exposition in 1937. I recorded with Coleman Hawkins—a prince!—and with Django Reinhardt and Stéphane Grappelli. And I got married for the first time. My wife was Sophia Mezzero, and she was a dancer and singer and pianist from Vienna. She died in Paris, in 1939, giving birth to my oldest son, Tommy. I was married again, in 1952, to Dorothy Morgan, and we had three children— Lisa, who's eighteen, Cynthia, who's sixteen, and Charles, who would be twenty-one. He was killed in the South Bronx when he was twenty, and for three days we didn't know he was dead. After Charles' death, we moved from the Bronx out to Mount Vernon. We live in a two-family house. Anyway, I was with Willie Lewis when the war broke out in Europe in 1939, and we made our way to Switzerland and into Spain and then Portugal, working all the time. I took Tommy, who was twenty-one months, to a bullfight in Madrid, and when the matador killed the bull Tommy applauded with everyone and sat down and then stood by himself and applauded again and the whole audience stood with him and clapped, too. We came back on the Exeter in October of 1941, and a German bomber flew right over us and everybody fell down on their knees and prayed. I moved in with one of my sisters in New York. I'd been away nine and a half years.

"I had come to New York in 1920. My first job was at a dance hall, the Garden of Joy, which was built on 'the rock,' at Seventh Avenue and a Hundred and Thirty-ninth Street. A saxophonist, name of Bob Fuller, had the band, and we followed Mamie Smith and Her Jazz Hounds. Coleman Hawkins was still with the Jazz Hounds, and that's when I met him. Harlem was full of piano players—Willie Gant and James P. Johnson and Willie the Lion Smith and Luckey Roberts and Fats Waller. The best of them was Fats. He played so clear and clean I never heard him hit a bad note. Then I went into a dime-a-dance place, the Rose Danceland, on a Hundred and Twenty-fifth Street. I believe Freddie Moore played there later. I shifted over to Marie Lucas at Goldgraben's, at a Hundred and Thirty-third and Lenox Avenue. She was Will Marion Cook's niece, and she played piano and trombone, and arranged and conducted. We jumped out of New York with her and into Washington, D.C. We had seven pieces and she added three, and one of them was Juan Tizol, who was with Duke Ellington later. After a couple of months, we went to the Smile-a-While Inn in Asbury Park and then to the Tent in Atlantic City. Jean Goldkette used to come in and conduct the band. Those were summer jobs, and in the fall we were hired into the Everglades Club, at Forty-eighth and Broadway. Ethel Waters was there, and Adelaide Hall, who lives in England, was her understudy. Edith Wilson sang, too, and—what!— she's still beautiful and can sing. Red Fletcher took over the band, and we went on the road to places like Binghamton and ended at the Metropolitan Burlesque, on Fourteenth Street. I jumped back to Marie Lucas—this was about 1925 or 1926—at the Hoofer's Club, which was under the La- fayette Theatre, at Seventh Avenue between a Hundred and Thirty-first and a Hundred and Thirty-second. Willie the Lion Smith came over from Newark, and he replaced Marie Lucas. He was a know-it-all who'd give people who didn't know him a fit. Chick Webb was in New York, and his uncle, George Young, had introduced us and asked me would I mind teaching him what I could. I let him sit in at the Hoofer's Club, and it used to drive Willie the Lion crazy, because Chick still didn't have it together. The best drummers in New York then were Walter Johnson and Kaiser Marshall and George Stafford and Old Man Brooks,

who was in the pit band at the Lafayette. Sid Catlett came in
1929 or 1930, and he was my main man. We used to swap
ideas, and if he got two jobs he'd give me one, and I'd do
the same. When we walked down the street together, I'd say
to him, 'Sid, you're too big. I don't want anyone to see
me lookin' so short next to you, so I'm going to walk in
front.' Later, we used to get on him all the time because
he never went to bed. We'd say, 'Why don't you go home
and get a good night's rest?' He was a terrific gambler, and
he'd say, 'Oh, man, I feel like I can make some money
tonight,' and he'd play cards into the next day and then
go to work. He just wore himself out is what killed him.

"I joined Charles Skeete at the Strand Ballroom, a dime-
a-dance in Brooklyn. I was there two or three years, then I
jumped to my brother Bill's band at a place on a Hundred
and Twenty-fifth. Jelly Roll Morton started coming in, and
he'd ask my brother if he could sit in and sing. He took a
liking to us and he'd bring his music and we'd run it down
right there. We had heard of him, but we didn't know how
good he was until he asked us to record with him for RCA
Victor. I guess we made about a dozen records between
1928 and 1930—titles like 'Fussy Mabel' and 'Pontchartrain'
and 'Boogaboo' and 'Mournful Serenade' and 'Little Lawrence.' Jelly Roll had brought Omer Simeon from Chicago,
and he was on some of them. So was Geechy Fields, and
Ward Pinkett, and Bubber Miley, who was with Duke
Ellington. Ellington couldn't stand Morton's music, but
Claude Hopkins couldn't stand Ellington's, so it equalled
out. Jelly Roll still had that diamond in his front tooth. He
bragged a lot, but I liked him. Anyway, we didn't have any
trouble with him. His music sounded old-fashioned at first,
but after a time you realized it was just a different kick.
You play his music now, of course, it sounds beautiful. I
worked a while for Wilbur de Paris during the fifties at
Jimmy Ryan's. I wouldn't have done it but for his brother
Sidney, who was a great trumpet player. People would give
us tips and Wilbur would always take them. One night, I
got twenty dollars and I waved it in front of him and then

put it in my pocket so he could see me doing it, and he didn't say a word. He fired me, because he wanted Zutty Singleton, and when Zutty only lasted three months Wilbur told me he wanted me back, but I was finished working with him. Zutty was a press-roll drummer, and all that rolling would tire his wrists and the tempo would slip some.

"After my brother's band, I went into the Alhambra Theatre with Edgar Hayes, and then I started rehearsing with Eddie South. We opened Ben Marden's Riviera, across the George Washington Bridge—which was brand-new. Paul Whiteman played opposite us, and he had Jack Teagarden and George Wettling. Milt Hinton came in with us on bass, and Everett Barksdale on guitar. Bing Crosby and Martha Raye worked there, too. I'd seen her sit in up in Harlem, and she was a very good singer and a hell of a dancer— what! Fats Waller needed a drummer, so I went on the road with him. He'd buy us drinks, but he always told us first, 'You get drunk on the bandstand, that'll mean your job.' He had Hank Duncan on piano, because he liked to get up and direct the band and clown around, and sometimes the two of them would play duets. Fats would order two or three meals at one sitting in a restaurant, and drinks to match, but I never saw him stagger one day in my life.

"I started out an orphan. I was the youngest of two boys and two girls. I never knew my mother, and my father died when I was five. He was a carpenter, and he played tuba and drums, which is odd, because that's what my brother Bill and I play. My father was William and my mother was Ann, and I've been told she played organ. When I was a baby, I was taken to an aunt, Lillian Campbell, in Charleston, South Carolina. Her husband was a tailor. Bill and I went there, and our sisters went with our father's sister. I believe we stayed at my aunt's two or three years, and when I was five and my brother eight were put in the Jenkins Orphanage, in the same city. It was a big brick building at No. 20 Franklin Street. The Reverend Dr. Jenkins was a wonderful person, and we were treated very well. They had three different bands, with twenty-five or so members in each. I started on the alto and baritone horns and the trombone, but it wasn't long before I went over to the drums. The bands played blues and overtures and marches, and they travelled all over the country giving concerts. We went to England in 1913, and played for the king and queen. When we got back, we were sent to rest at a farm upstate that the Reverend Jenkins had. Musically, they started you right at the bottom at the orphanage and worked you up through the rudiments until you knew your instrument backward and forward. Some first-rate musicians came out of the orphanage—my brother Bill, Gus Aiken, who played trumpet with Sidney Bechet, Cat Anderson, who was with Duke Ellington so long, and Jabbo Smith, who recorded with Ellington and had Chicago on its head in 1929 with his trumpet playing. People say he was the first Dizzy Gillespie, and they're right. When I was sixteen, I ran away from the orphanage. We knew about the money that musicians were making on the outside, and we wanted some. Bill and I ran away, and we got ourselves to Virginia, where we joined a minstrel show called Green River. Then we went with a doctor show, where the man sold patent medicines. We'd play two or three tunes, the man would talk about his medicines, and we'd play another selection while the people paid up. He had his own bus, and we travelled in that. The orphanage caught up with us in Georgia. We stayed two or three months, and ran away again. I got a job in a hotel in Charleston as a bellhop, and we joined a circus and stayed six months, until it reached Cincinnati. We played in the band. Bill went to New York, and I got a job in the pit band at the Lincoln Theatre. The blues singers all came through, and one of them was Jackie Mabley, who became Moms Mabley. I stayed three or four months, then went on to Chicago for a couple of years. I was in a band at the Columbia Tavern, at Thirty-first and State, led by a violinist named Brownie. Happy Caldwell, the tenor saxophonist, was in that band. We heard King Oliver's Creole Jazz Band, and it was beautiful. It was a loud band, and Johnny Dodds was the main soloist. Those New Orleans

musicians played a lot of slow blues and medium tunes, and
when they went to New York they were amazed because
New York musicians played so fast. The New Orleans
drummers used press rolls all the time, and sometimes they
sounded like they were just going to slow down and stop.
I heard Freddie Keppard, and I didn't care for him too
much, but Sammy Stewart, who brought Sid Catlett to New
York, had a very good band. And Earl Hines was knocking
everybody out. Then I jumped out of Chicago with a show
that played Indianapolis and Pittsburgh and ended in New
York, where I moved in with my brother and his wife. I already knew it didn't matter where I was. When I'm behind
my drums, I'm home."

Freddie Moore looks like Erich von Stroheim. He is bald
and short, and has powerful brown eyes. His skin is tight
and smooth, and he has an invincible voice. Many of the
older drummers grew up in vaudeville, and they come in
two parts—the showman and the musician. Like Benford,
Moore learned much of what he knows as a minstrel-band
drummer around the time of the First World War. There
were no microphones, and the performers worked more
in shadow than in light. Exaggeration got their acts across:
singers were loud, comedians were hammy, and musicians
were exhibitionistic. Moore still uses the showoff stuff he
picked up sixty years ago. He pops his eyes on the final beat
of a tune, and makes them roll when he sings, which he
does in a hopsack, over-the-mountain voice. Before his vocal
on "Ugly Chile," he puts on a horrendous orange wig and
dark glasses with white frames, and on "Tiger Rag," in the
strain where the trombone makes tiger-roar noises, he turns
his snare drum over and blows like a demon on the wire
snares, producing a wild wind-tunnel sound. He also takes
a drum solo in which he uses five sticks. He begins with a
stick held pirate fashion in his teeth, one under each arm,
and one in each hand. As he plays, he rapidly revolves
them—the stick in his mouth moves under his right arm, the

one under his right arm goes into his right hand, the one in his right hand is switched to his left, the one in his left goes under his left arm, and the one under his left arm is clamped in his teeth—without losing a beat. All the while, he flashes his eyes and shakes his lips, and the whole is phantasmagoric. ("When you get tired of drummin'," he says, "you start clownin'.") Moore is also a solid, driving drummer of a kind almost gone. He favors press rolls and a single, heavy cymbal beat, and his rimshots splinter and crack. There is no subtlety in his playing, nor is there any hesitation or confusion. You could build a house on his beat. He works about three nights a week, and that's all he cares to handle. He lives in a housing development in the Bronx with his wife, Lucille, whom he married in 1941. He is a serious, steadfast talker, and his rare smiles are startling. After he had set up his drums for a gig at One Fifth Avenue one Friday, he talked:

"Fred Moore was born August 20, 1900, in Little Washington, North Carolina. I had three sisters and three brothers, and I was the baby. I don't know much about my father outside of his name, Giles Moore, because he died when I was nine weeks old. My mother was Hattie Moore. She was short, and part Cherokee. When I was little, she moved us all to New Bern, North Carolina, which was about forty miles south. Later, I got my limp by trying to snag a caboose to go visit Little Washington and getting my foot caught between the ties and tearing my knee. I did about four years in school. As long as I can remember, I wanted to be a drummer. There was a place called the Frog Pond, where they had dances and a piano player and a drummer. The piano player's name was Hootie Green, and he played stride and boogie-woogie. I don't recall the drummer's name, but I paid him a dime when I had the money to let me sit in on his drums, and I'd get up there and hit anything and not make any sense at all. I practiced on boxes and chairs and table legs around the house, but my mother didn't care for that, so when I was fourteen I ran away. I went with the A. G. Allen minstrel show. It travelled by train, and they kept the tent for the show in the parson's belly—under a car. The show had an eight-piece band, and an old-time comedian who blacked his face and put white on his lips, a soubrette, and six chorus girls. We ate beef stew and potatoes, collard greens, ribs, neck bones, and beans and rice. When we got to a new town and they were unpacking and setting up the tent, the band would get into its clothes, which were long red coats, fezzes, and dickeys with wing collars. The band would march around the town to announce the show, and sometimes it would cover three or four miles. I was called 'the walking gent.' I'd walk right alongside the drummer, watching him, and when the march was finished and the band all in a sweat it was my job to spread their coats out on bushes and on the grass so they'd be dry for the first show. During the shows, I'd sit and watch the drummer, and that way I learned. When I'd been with the show three months, the drummer took sick and they asked me could I play. I didn't know if I could or not, but I was young and wil', young and fly, so I played the show. I'd been getting three dollars a week, and by the time I quit the show, four months later, I was making twenty dollars.

"I got a job in Birmingham, Alabama, playing with an organist for the silent pictures. When new pictures came, I'd go down in the morning and rehearse, so that I'd know where the thunder and lightning was and the gunshots and the stampedes. I stayed in Birmingham about seven years, and besides the moving pictures I played for attractions who came through—Ida Cox, and Bessie Smith, who was shorter than you expected and not too fat, and Sara Martin, and Ma Rainey. Ma Rainey was some ugly. She had a diamond in a lower front tooth and a twenty-dollar gold piece hanging down her front and a ten-dollar gold piece on each ear. She sang songs you never heard other singers do, and I'd say she was between a blues singer and a folk singer. She used her hands a lot. Mamie Smith came through, too, and she had the trumpeter Johnny Dunn, who was the first I ever heard use the plunger mute. I left Birmingham with the

William Benbow show, and we worked Macon, Georgia, and Havana, Cuba, and we ended up at the Savoy Theatre in Detroit, Michigan. It had six balconies and sat three thousand people. After a while, I put together my own seven-piece band—Buddy Moore and His Carolina Stompers. They had got to calling me Buddy with A. G. Allen, and I hadn't changed to my real name yet. We played what we called 'swing' music—not 'Dixieland,' which was a term we had never heard. In 1928, I came to New York. I had saved my money, and I had a few dollars. The first night, I spent about fifty dollars buying drinks, paying my way in. I heard Chick Webb at the Rose Danceland, and I'm telling you that shut me up a little. The next night, I heard Cozy Cole, who was a tame drummer, at the Primrose Dance Land, and a couple of nights later I heard Tommy Benford. He was smooth, and made the band feel good and happy. I worked at the Lafayette Theatre with Wilbur Sweatman, and then I went into the pit band of Eubie Blake's 'Shuffle Along,' at fifty-five dollars a week. I recorded with King Oliver in 1930, and went on the road with him in 1931. He was a sweet man. I think people wanted him to blow up a storm, but his gums were bad and he couldn't make those arrangements, and, maybe because of that, we didn't do so good. He was offered the chance to open at the Grand Terrace in Chicago, but he wanted too much money, and Earl Hines went in instead and stayed off and on for about ten years. We called Oliver Google-Eye behind his back, because one eye was almost shut from some accident. He didn't drink, but he'd sit down and eat a loaf of light bread and a whole fried chicken, and drink two quarts of milk and a pitcher of ice water with plenty of sugar in it.

"When I saw that the tour wasn't going anywhere and Oliver had no notion of returning to New York right away, I left and came back and got me a little band at the Victoria Café, at a Hundred and Forty-first and Seventh Avenue. I had Pete Brown on alto saxophone and Don Frye on piano. All the white musicians from downtown—Tommy Dorsey and Gene Krupa and Jack Teagarden—would sit in after work, and they'd still be there at ten in the morning. Then we went into the One-Hundred-One Ranch Club, at a Hundred and Thirty-ninth and Lenox Avenue, and from there into the Brittwood club, where John Kirby took over the band. He brought along Buster Bailey and Chu Berry and Frankie Newton. It was too much of a clique, and I didn't want that. They didn't want me, either. Kirby fired me, and then he fired Pete Brown, and then Frye, and we ended up back at the Victoria. I was with Edgar Hayes a while, and I spent three or four years at the Circle Ballroom, at Fifty-eighth and Eighth. It was a taxi-dance place. Every time I hit the wood block, the customer would have to give the girl another ticket, and sometimes one ticket only lasted two choruses. I went into the Village Vanguard with Max Kaminsky and Art Hodes in 1939, and we stayed a few years. I played the Sunday-afternoon jam sessions at the old Jimmy Ryan's in the forties, and in the fifties I was house drummer at the Stuyvesant Casino, on Second Avenue. I also worked for a spell with Wilbur de Paris. I consider myself very fortunate. I've worked all my life. A lot of people have asked me to get my own band, but I don't want the headaches. Same time, I can't ever stop playing. If I did, I'd fall dead."

Sonny Greer is an elegant pipestem, with a narrow, handsome face and flat black hair. His eyes are lustrous, and his fingers are long and spidery. He was with Duke Ellington for almost thirty years, and sat godlike above and behind the band, surrounded by a huge, white, blazing set of drums. He played with vigor and snap. He switched his head from side to side to accent beats and, his trunk a post, windmilled his arms. His cymbals dipped and reflected his sudden smiles. His playing was homemade and unique, and he isn't sure himself where it came from. He used timpani and tomtoms a lot, filling cracks and cheering the soloists. He used deceptive, easy arrays of afterbeat rimshots that drove the band while remaining signals of cool. He flicked cowbells to launch a soloist, and he showered everyone with cymbals. He sparkled and exploded, but his taste never faltered. He and Ellington set the streamlined, dicty tone of the band; after Greer left, the band never fully recovered. Ellington didn't care for drum solos, but Greer takes a lot of two-bar breaks on "Jumpin' Punkins," and during a soundie (a three-minute film made to be shown on a jukebox equipped with a small screen) Greer takes a crackling, expert double-timing twelve-bar solo on "C Jam Blues" which matches his idol, Sid Catlett. Greer goes in and out of retirement every few months; when he works, it is with Brooks Kerr, the twenty-seven-year-old pianist, singer, and repository of Ellingtonia. Greer lives in a new building on Central Park West with his wife, Millicent, who was a Cotton Club dancer when he married her, fifty-two years ago. They have one daughter, and a granddaughter who is a vice-president of a bank in Omaha. Greer's life has been distilled in his mind into a collection of tales that are elastic, embroidered, interchangeable. He likes to tell them in the same way he plays the drums—with poppings of his eyes and quick, geometric gestures. His voice is low and hoarse, his speech legato. He often sits at his dining-room table and talks, his back to a window, his face alternately smiling and straight. He remembers his own dictum "When you're getting ready to lie, don't smile." He talked one afternoon, the day after he'd played a party with Brooks Kerr:

"I first met Duke Ellington and Toby Hardwicke on a corner in front of a restaurant near the Howard Theatre in Washington, D.C., and they asked me what New York was like, and I painted a beautiful picture for them. I liked Duke and Toby right away, and we were inseparable the next thirty years. I first took them to New York on March 10, 1921—Toby, Duke, Artie Whetsol, and Elmer Snowden—and when we got there the booker said he wanted names, so the job collapsed. I introduced them around—to James P. Johnson and Luckey Roberts and so forth—and if I didn't know somebody I introduced them anyway. New York amazed them—all the music you could desire, and much more. We got jobs playing house-rent parties—one dollar plus eats. We ran into Bricktop on Seventh Avenue. She was the chanteuse at Barron Wilkins', and she helped us out. We played a lot of pool. We survived. We ended up back in Washington, but when we returned to New York, in 1923, we went into the Kentucky Club, at Forty-ninth and Broadway, and we were there three or four years. It was a basement club, and if a revenue agent came around the doorman stepped on a foot buzzer and the place turned into a church. Johnny Hudgins, who did pantomime, was in the show, and so was the trumpeter Joe Smith, who made talking sounds on his horn with his hands. Fats Waller was in the show, along with singers and dancers. People like Texas Guinan and Polly Adler came in. Duke and I played a party for Polly Adler once. Fats would sit at a little piano in the middle of the floor, and I'd sing risky songs with him. When Leo Bernstein, who was one of the owners, got plastered, he'd ask me for 'My Buddy.' I'd sing a long version, and he'd start crying and tell me he wanted to give me the joint and everything else he had. We went from there into the Cotton Club, where Duke and the band began to be world famous.

"I made a deal back then with the Leedy drum people, in Elkhart, Indiana. In return for my posing for publicity shots and giving testimonials, they gave me a drum set that was the most beautiful in the world. Drummers would come up to me and say, 'Sonny, where did you get those drums? You must be rich, man,' and I'd nod. I had two timpani, chimes, three tomtoms, a bass drum, a snare—the initials S.G. painted on every drum—five or six cymbals, temple blocks, a cowbell, wood blocks, gongs of several sizes, and a vibraphone. The cymbals were from the Zildjian factory. I'd go out to Quincy when we were working in the Boston area, and one of the Zildjians would take me around. He'd tell me to choose cymbals with flat cups—that's the raised portion at the center—and instead of hitting a cymbal to show me how it sounded he'd pinch the edge with his fingers, and you could tell just by the ring. I learned how to keep my drums crisp, to tune them so they had an even, clear sound. I knew about showmanship, about how audiences eat it up—that it ain't what you do but how you do it. Things like hitting three rimshots and opening and closing one side of my jacket in time. I always strove for delicacy. I always tried to shade and make everything sound beautiful. It was my job to keep the band in level time, to keep slow tempos from going down and fast tempos from going up. Those things meant more to me than solos, which I rarely took.

"My parents taught me that way of caring. I was born December 13, 1902, in Long Branch, New Jersey, which is just this side of Asbury Park. My mother was a modiste. She copied original gowns for wealthy white people. She was tall and had a charming personality. My father was about the same height and he was a master electrician with the Pennsylvania Railroad, and his greatest ambition was for me to follow in his footsteps. There were four children— Saretta, who was the oldest, then me, and Madeline, and my brother Eddie. I was named after my father—William Alexander Greer, Jr. I was interested in the affection our parents showed us, but beyond that our life was an everyday occasion, except that we never went hungry a day. I always had an ambition to make an honest dollar, to make money and not have money make me, and that's the way it's been. When I was twelve, I'd take my homemade wagon and load up at the fish place after school for fifty cents—cod, blowfish, blues, bass. My customers would wait for me on corners, and some of those fish were so big you had to bake them. I also had a paper route, and I delivered groceries. My first love was playing pool, ten cents a game. I practiced pool like other kids practice violin or piano. I'd practice two hours a day. I'd hide a pair of long pants, and after school put them on and go to the poolroom. I had a natural knack for it. Nobody in my family was musically inclined, including me, so my becoming a drummer was an accident—a hidden talent. We had Keith vaudeville in Long Branch, and when J. Rosamond Johnson brought his company through he had a drummer named Peggy Holland—Eugene

Holland. He was tall and thin and immaculate—the picture of sartorial splendor. He could sing and dance and play, and he had great delicacy. He fascinated me. The company was in town two weeks, and every time he came into the poolroom I'd beat him. I told him I admired his playing, and he said, 'Kid, teach me to play pool like you play, and I'll do the same for you.' I bought him a box of cigars just to put an edge on it, and he gave me six or seven lessons, and some of the things he showed me I still use. I went to the Chattle High School, where they had a twenty-five-piece band. Mme. Briskie was in charge of it. She also taught languages, at which I was very good. I didn't think the drummer was too hot, so I told Mme. Briskie, 'I can beat that guy playing.' I gave her a light taste, then I poured a march on her, and all the kids watching were prancing. I got the job. I could sing, too—like a mockingbird. We put together a small band, and it had six white boys, two white girl singers, and me, the Indian. Jersey was like Georgia then, it was so prejudiced, and I was learning how to look trouble in the face. Along with my other money-making enterprises, I was a first-class caddie, and for a year I'd been the personal caddie to one of the daughters of Krueger Beer. One day, she sliced a ball into a water hazard, and when I got there I laid the bag of clubs down and started into the water. Then I saw that a snake had that ball in his mouth, and I said, 'Oh, no.' She got mad and I quit and walked away and left her there, bag and all. Later that summer, our little band played a dance at the country club where she played golf, and she was sitting at ringside. She kept looking at me—she could hardly help it, because I was the sore thumb—and asking who I was. Finally, she asked me, 'Don't I know you? Didn't you used to caddie for me?' I told her, 'No'm. Not me. That was my twin brother.' She didn't find out the truth until I met her backstage years later at Carnegie Hall after an Ellington concert.

"I left high school the year before graduation, and that broke my parents' hearts. But my soul was set on the music. Sundays, I used to go up to New York for rehearsals at the

Clef Club with Will Marion Cook, who had a lot of Lester Lanin-type bands. My mother asked me what we were rehearsing for, and I said, 'A trip to Russia.' She said, 'A trip to *what?* That's it! No more rehearsing!' When I was around nineteen, I played in the Plaza Hotel on the boardwalk at Asbury Park. Fats Waller was on piano and Shrimp Jones on violin. A string ensemble called the Conaway Brothers worked there, too, and I became friendly with them. They were from Washington, D.C., and they invited me down for three days, and I stayed several years. Marie Lucas had a band at the Howard Theatre, and one morning the manager came into the poolroom next door and said Marie Lucas needed a drummer, since hers had run off to Canada with the alimony agents after him. That was my first Washington engagement. The bootleggers had the habit of stacking money on a table for the entertainers who worked at the Dreamland Café, around the corner from the Howard. Soon I was doubling there with Claude Hopkins and Harry White from midnight until six in the morning, and after we collected our money from that table we had so much in our pockets it was a sin.

"Duke Ellington was like my brother, and I was like his. He was once-in-a-lifetime, and I wish I had a third of his personality. It overshadowed everybody else. He was sharp as a Gillette blade. His mother and father drilled that into him—Uncle Ed and Aunt Daisy, we used to call them. His father was a fine-looking man, and *polished.* Duke learned his way of talking from Uncle Ed. Fact, his father taught him everything he knew. Duke would never let a guy associated with the band down, no matter what hour of the day or night the trouble might be. He couldn't tolerate dissension in the band, or trouble from a new guy. He could sense right away when a guy wasn't right. But he never had a mean streak in his life. Duke was sort of a dreamer. Even when he'd play cards with us on the train, he'd have a song or a piece of music going through his head. *That* was his life. Every tick of the clock, somebody in the world is playing an Ellington tune.

"We first went to Europe in 1933—right from the Cotton Club. We went directly to London, where we played the Palladium. After, we did a party for Lord Beaverbrook—champagne and brandy in front of every one of us. I poured a glass of each to get my nerves together. Anna May Wong was a guest, and Jeannette MacDonald, and the future King George. He sat in on piano, and he and Duke played duets. Then I noticed this skinny little guy squatting near the drums and watching me, and pretty soon he asks can we play 'The Charleston.' We did, and he danced like crazy. Then he asked me could he sit in on drums, and I said, 'Of course, my man.' Somebody told me who he was: the Prince of Wales. I christened him the Whale, and it stuck. After I'd left the Duke, in the fifties, he came across the street from El Morocco to the Embers, where I was working, and I called him the Whale, and we sat and talked and told a few lies.

"By the early forties, the band was a bunch of admired stars, each with a different style. Johnny Hodges was very even-mannered. He was a thoroughbred. Whenever you'd wake Toby Hardwicke up, he was ready to go. But Ben Webster was the *king* of the playboys. We called him Frog, or the Brute, even though he was most congenial. Cootie Williams liked to gamble, but he didn't drink much. Lawrence Brown didn't drink, either, but he loved the ladies. Tricky Sam Nanton—he and Ben Webster and Toby were all in the same category: curiosity always got the better of them. Jimmy Blanton was a lovely boy, and he was crazy about his instrument. He'd stay up with us all night just to hear other people play. Ben was his umbrella and watched out for him. Ray Nance was a cocky kid, and we called him the Captain. He was always ready when asked—'Just a minute, I'll be right with you.' Barney Bigard was the best, and here is how he got his nickname—Creole. Once, when we were down South and in a bus on our way back to our Pullman car after a job, we stopped at a greasy spoon to get something to eat. Duke sent Bigard and Wellman Braud in, because they looked practically white. They were in there a long time before the door banged open and Barney came out shouting, 'I'm Creole! I'm Creole!' The owner of the place was right behind him, waving and shouting back, 'I don't care how old you are, you can't eat in here!' We travelled by Pullman before the war—one car to sleep and eat in, and one car for our instruments and baggage. That way, we didn't have to face the enmity of looking for a place to stay. No other band travelled as well or looked as well. If we did six shows a day in a theatre, we changed our clothes six times.

"I feel good, and I can still play. Lazy people retire. As long as you feel active, *be* active. Retired people lie under a tree and play checkers, and first thing you know they're gone. Last time I saw Duke in the hospital, he said, 'I want you to go out and play again, Nasty.' He called me that because I had always defended him against all comers through the years. Shortly after, I started working with Brooks Kerr, and I'm still working with him. I guess the Man isn't ready for me yet. The only regret I have is that my parents and my sisters never saw me play with the Duke Ellington band. My brother Eddie did, but somehow they didn't, and I'm still sorry about that."

Starting at the Top

Jabbo Smith was born in 1908, and he has been a legend half his life. Or, to put it another way, he was only in his mid-thirties when he began to slide into obscurity. At seventeen, he joined Charle Johnson's excellent band, and within a year he had the New York brass establishment on its ear. Just short of nineteen, he recorded two spectacular takes of "Black and Tan Fantasy" with Duke Ellington and was asked by Ellington to join his band. Full of oats, Smith turned Ellington down. Four months later, he joined James P. Johnson and Fats Waller in the "Keep Shufflin'" band, and recorded four classic Victor sides with Johnson, Waller, and the reedman Garvin Bushell. The show closed in Chicago late in 1928, and Smith stayed put. He gave Louis Armstrong an ecstatic run for his money by recording nineteen small-band sides for the Brunswick label, which are still startling. His career, just five years old, began to slow down, and after a two-year stint with Claude Hopkins (1936-38) and a spell at the New York World's Fair (1939) he vanished. By the mid-forties, he had settled in Milwaukee, and by the mid-fifties he was out of music. His legend had formed. In 1953, the English *Jazz Journal* began a search for Smith. Two years later, the bassist Milt Hinton was quoted by Nat Hentoff and Nat Shapiro in their oral history "Hear Me Talkin' to Ya": "Jabbo was as good as Louis [in 1930]. He was the Dizzy Gillespie of that era. He played rapid-fire passages while Louis was melodic and beautiful . . . He could play soft and he could play fast but he never made it. He got hung up in Newark . . . He had delusions of grandeur and he'd always get mixed up with women . . . If he made enough for drinks and chicks in any small town like Des Moines or Milwaukee, that would suffice." A painter named Phil Stein heard Smith when we was hung up in Newark. "I was a member of the Newark Hot Club," Stein has said, "and we used to go into the black section all the time looking for rare recordings. We also went into the black bars that had music, and we went enough so that we became accepted. One night in 1941, we stopped at the Alcazar, and there was a blues group, playing very easy. It had an interesting trumpet player, rather muffled and subdued, but it was so dark we couldn't tell who it was. When we learned it was Jabbo Smith, we couldn't believe it. We knew all his Brunswicks and his four Deccas. We spoke to him immediately, and discovered that he was kind of down and out. He was sickly and his lip was bad, and he had a miserable room in a boarding house. We visited him there, and he had all these pencil portraits of himself. He said he wanted to be an artist. He seemed to me a very introverted person, very frail, a poetic kind of person. We were concerned with trying to pull him up, so we organized a little concert for him to raise some money, but it wasn't a success. He did go back with Claude Hopkins for a while, and we went to see him in his apartment after he moved to Harlem, but then the war came along, and the next I knew the *Jazz Journal* was looking for him."

In 1961, Roy Eldridge, Sammy Price, and Jo Jones had this conversation:

"I saw [Jabbo Smith] two years ago in Newark," Eldridge said to Price. "And he was playing trombone, too!"

"Jabbo Smith?" Price exclaimed. "Why, he's dead, man! Here, I'll bet you a hundred dollars."

"Dead? He lives in Milwaukee," Jones said . . . "I've got his address right in my book."

"Put up your money," Price said to Eldridge.

In 1968, Gunther Schuller gave five admiring pages to Smith in "Early Jazz," pointing out along the way that Smith was indeed living in Milwaukee, where he worked for a car-rental company. Three years later, the trumpeter made the first of several visits to Europe, and he was heard by the Swedish clarinettist Orange Kellin, who urged him to move to New Orleans, where Kellin said he could get him work. Smith eventually went. He played briefly at Preservation Hall, and then joined the band in the musical "One Mo' Time."

Jazz categorists have long declared Jabbo Smith a second-rate Louis Armstrong, which is like calling Scott Fitzgerald a follower of Hemingway. Armstrong was guided by rhythmic and melodic considerations, but Smith was directed largely by technique. Armstrong was lyrical and poetic: he tacked along in the sun behind the beat, and he created arching, supernal melodies. He was able to say beautifully everything he had in his mind. When he made occasional nonsense forays into his highest register, it destroyed the serene balance of his style. Smith's style was never completely balanced. He kept poking at his technical boundaries, playing high notes and wild intervals and thirty-second-note runs that had never been played before. This was particularly true after he arrived in Chicago and challenged Armstrong, whom he had known only from recordings. Before that, in New York, Smith's playing was sly and sinuous and lyrical. It was the first cool jazz improvisation. There was little straining for effect, and the surprises were quiet and steady. He preferred the silver forests around high C, and his high notes, almost all of them quick and glancing, gave his playing a subtle urgency. He played with smoothness and aplomb, and there are passages in " 'Sippi" and "Thou Swell," recorded with Fats Waller, Garvin Bushell, and James P. Johnson, where he displays the dancing ease of Charlie Shavers. In Chicago, the shadow of Louis Armstrong seems to have unnerved him. He grew agitated on the Brunswick recordings, and his once creamy melodic lines jump and zigzag. He misses notes, and he blares. He goes after intervals and arpeggios that Armstrong couldn't have managed, either. He shows off. The Brunswick records were designed to compete with Armstrong's successful Hot Fives and Hot Sevens. The instrumentation of trumpet, clarinet, piano, banjo, and bass is similar, and there are many passages where Smith sounds as if he were consciously imitating Armstrong. ("Croonin' the Blues" is a rough copy of "West End Blues.") But the New York Jabbo keeps breaking through, and is there on "Sweet and Low Blues," "Tanguay Blues," "Decatur St. Tutti," and "Boston Skuffle." His dynamics are superb (two muted choruses on "Tanguay Blues"), he is leaping and mercurial, he is full of sorrowing blue notes, and he delivers several scat-sung vocals that surpass Armstrong. There are many intimations: Roy Eldridge breaks; legato passages that suggest the Henry Allen of 1933; fast muted runs ("Sweet and Low Blues") that resemble Dizzy Gillespie. The Brunswicks are among the best of the early jazz recordings.

Jabbo Smith is of medium height, and has the flat, rectangular look of thin older men. He is very dark, and this tends to minimize his features, which are strong—a square chin, high cheekbones, widely spaced eyes, and a broad, trellised forehead. His fingers are thick and strong. His speech rises and falls rapidly, and some of his sentences are opaque: the words move by without pause, and meaning goes under. He has a rapid, jouncing laugh. The cocksure twenty-year-old trumpet player who set out to dethrone Louis Armstrong is no longer visible, but now and then he peers out from behind the blinds. Smith talked one afternoon:

"To me, all this is beautiful. My chops are getting better and better working every night, and within a month or so my playing should make pretty good sense. Of course, if I hadn't laid off twenty years I'd probably be burned out now. I've always had lip trouble. We were taught to use a lot of pressure when I started out—pressing the mouthpiece against your upper lip real hard—which cut off the circulation and made all kinds of problems. They don't teach that anymore, and that's probably why trumpet players can go so high now—high enough so you don't even know what notes they're playing. The ability to improvise has never left me. I keep the melody in my mind, and I don't think about the chords, which you're supposed to know anyway. You never have too much time to think, but things always come to you—little melodic things that sound good and add decoration. What I like to do is paint the melody. My aspiration is also to be a songwriter. I've written about two hundred songs, and I'm betting on those. The two songs I sing in the show—'Love' and 'Yes, Yes'—are mine.

"The show is supposed to be set in the twenties, and it's not that different from 'Keep Shufflin',' which I joined in 1928. James P. Johnson had the band, and Fats Waller was in it. Fats was a beautiful personality, just like he was on the stand. James P. was more calm. But they were night-and-day buddies. After the show closed, I became the house trumpeter at the Sunset Café, and, of course, I met Louis Armstrong. Louis was with Carroll Dickerson, and he was playing things like 'West End Blues.' I sat in with him, and I don't think anybody won. We played different styles. He was more melodic, and I played running horn, with a lot of notes. He and Zutty Singleton were fabulous people. We'd meet here and there, and one time Louis talked about him and me teaming up together, but nothing came of it. Early in January, 1929, I recorded with the banjo player Ikey Robinson, and Mayor Williams, who was booking the race talent for the Brunswick label, heard me and asked me to make some records under my own name. I used Ikey and Omer Simeon, who had worked with King Oliver and Jelly

Roll Morton. I also had a piano and bass, and we did almost twenty sides that year, and they didn't go *any*where. They've been reissued, though, and people tell me they're doing a lot better now than when they first came out. I worked with everybody in Chicago—Erskine Tate and Dave Peyton and Charles Elgar, and with Tiny Parham and Jimmy Bell and Burns Campbell. I didn't meet Oliver until I was passing through Savannah in 1937, a year before he died. I was standing in the street talking to someone, and he came by. All I recall is that he was quiet and looked like an old man. Around 1930, I began moving back and forth between Milwaukee and Chicago, with side trips to Detroit. You get in a little trouble in Chicago, you run to Milwaukee; you get in a little trouble in Milwaukee, you run to Chicago. I had my own eight-piece band off and on for six years at the Wisconsin Roof in Milwaukee. I worked with Jesse Stone—Jesse Stone's Cyclones—and he had a lot of violins and people playing bottles with spoons. In 1936, I was at the Norwood Hotel in Detroit, and Pete Jacobs, the drummer, came running out of a restaurant shouting my name. He was with Claude Hopkins' big band, and they were inside eating and had seen me go by. Claude asked me to join him, and I did, in New York. It was a very good band. Jerry Blake was in it, and the trombonist Fred Norman and the singer Orlando Robeson. We spent a lot of time at the Roseland Ballroom, so we didn't have all that bouncing from town to town. But we made up for it when we did go on the road. We'd go from Waltham, Massachusetts, to Detroit to Chicago and back to Waltham in four days, and once, when we were booked into Charleston, West Virginia, Claude had a run-in with the gent who hired us. Claude was pretty haughty, and he said no to the man after he asked us to ride around in a truck playing and ballyhooing our performance. The man gave us fifteen minutes to get out of town. I left Claude in St. Louis, and went back to New York and took a little band into the Midway Inn at the World's Fair. Then I was at the Alcazar in Newark, first with my own band, and later with Larry Ringold's. We played for shows and dancing. I moved to Milwaukee for good in the forties, and worked on and off until the fifties, when I quit music and went to work for Avis. I have a house, and I'm married to a girl from South Dakota named Willie Mae, and I have two grown daughters in California. I don't know why I missed the big time, except you get tied up with those girls and things and you stay where you're most comfortable. Also, it doesn't help to start at the top, which was where I was by the time I was eighteen or nineteen.

"I was born the day before Christmas, in Pembroke, Georgia. I had a cousin born the same time, and her mother named her Gladys. On account of that, and since my mother was a schoolteacher and intellectual, she named me *Cladys*. Jabbo was hung on me later by a friend named James Reddick. He had been given the name after an ugly Indian in a William S. Hart movie, and he passed it on to me. My father was a barber, but I don't have any recollection of him. My mother took me to Savannah when I was four, which was about when my memory started working. My mother was a nice-looking person, about my height, with an Indian cast to her face. She played the organ in church, and before she was a teacher she worked cleaning Pullman cars. She couldn't take care of me, too, and I was all over Savannah, which was why she decided to put me in the Jenkins Orphanage, in Charleston, South Carolina. That was in 1914. She took me up on a Pullman, because they rode her free, and I cried for three months after I got there. The orphanage was famous all over that part of the South. Mothers used it as a weapon: 'You watch out, now, or I'll send you to Jenkins!' It had been started by the Reverend D. J. Jenkins, and it had already turned out about three thousand kids. Kids used to come to his house begging for food, and he found out they were living in boxcars and suchlike, so he'd take them in, and the word spread about his kindliness, and pretty soon he had quite a few children on his hands. The city of Charleston gave him the old Marine Hospital, and he started the orphanage. Eventually, the state gave him two hundred dollars a year to help out. He was a stately man with a beard, and he looked seventy or eighty to me, but I don't think he could have been that old. There were four hundred kids at Jenkin, and we did pretty well. We had a two-hundred-and-ninety-acre farm upstate, where we grew all our food, and we'd get day-old bread that had been saved in barrels at stores, and we'd get leftover fish down at the docks. We'd have molasses and bread at supper. Jenkins was strict. At six o'clock in the morning, there would be a prayer meeting, and after that the roll would be read, and if you did anything bad the day before you'd be called up and tied to a post and whipped with a rope or a piece of rein. To raise money for the orphanage, the Reverend Jenkins organized bands of maybe twelve kids each, eight to twelve in age, and we'd play on the street corners and pass the hat. We played on street corners all over Charleston, and we'd get sent to New York and Jacksonville and Savannah and suchlike to do the same. We also gave concerts at the churches in those places, at eight o'clock in the evening. On the street corners, it was every tub on its own bottom, every kid doing his own thing. All you needed to know was the melody, and then you'd take off from there. They've been saying all these years that jazz started in New Orleans, and all that, but what were we doing? Of course, when we performed in the churches it was overtures and marches. We stayed three months in New York once, and we went out and played on street corners all over New Jersey and Pennsylvania. We lived the whole time in two rooms in a rooming house at a Hundred and Thirty-third Street and Fifth Avenue, and the people that ran the place must have had a bellyful of us.

"At Jenkins, they started you in playing when you were about eight years old. The orphanage took children from the cradle, and the little ones stayed in the yard and were called yard boys. When the time came to learn an instrument, the teacher would come out in the yard and call, 'You!

Come here! *You!* Come here!' They taught everybody in the same room. They started me on the trumpet, but I learned to manage all the brass instruments. And they taught you to read right off. Musicians were already amazed later that I could read anything at sight. The trumpet player Gus Aiken, who was older, had run away to New York and played there, and when he was brought back I picked up things from him, too. I started running away when I was fourteen, and I must have run away six or seven times. When they put you in the orphanage, they signed you up until you were twenty-one, so running away was the only method to get out earlier. The first time I took off was in Jacksonville. When we travelled to New York or Jacksonville, we went by boat, and this time, marching back to the boat in line double-breasted, like we marched everywhere, James Reddick and I took off around a corner. We stayed with a boy in Jacksonville we knew, and we lived on money we had knocked down. 'Knocking down' was keeping a little of what we collected in the hat when we played in the street. I was already a wild kid, and I got a job with Eagle Eye Shields' band. I was pretty good, and people thought maybe I was going to be somebody. Shields had twelve in the band, and it was the first large band I'd played in. When you ran away, Jenkins notified the police, and they caught us after three months. They called me the ringleader, and I got three days in a cell, but it wasn't long before I ran away again.

"When I was sixteen, I got in real trouble. Some of my buddies—Reddick and Timothy and Mike and two brothers we called Perry No. 1 and Perry No. 2—had gone over to South Carolina State College, in Orangeburg, and I wanted to play in their band. I hadn't been there long before I accidentally shot myself in the leg with a pistol I'd picked up— just fooling around, and not knowing there was still a bullet in the chamber. They fixed me up and sent me back to the orphanage, and the Reverend Jenkins took me up on the veranda and said he'd done all he could for me—that they couldn't keep me any longer, because I was too wild. He gave me nine dollars in an envelope to go to Savannah, where my mother still lived. But I wanted to go North. I had run away to Philadelphia before, and my older half sister lived there, so I got on a train with my crutches and went to stay with her. I auditioned at the Waltz Dream Ballroom for Harry Marsh's band, and I was with him three months. Then I went to Atlantic City and ran into Gus Aiken, who was with the Drake and Walker Show, and I joined them for a month. I went back to Atlantic City, and met Charlie Johnson, and he said he wanted me. It was 1925, and Charlie Johnson had the best band in New York. It had Sidney de Paris, who was my idol. I liked the way he blew his horn and the way he used mutes. I never acquired his style, but he influenced me. Johnson also had Benny Carter and Edgar Sampson and Charlie Irvis and the great drummer George Stafford. I had a pretty good notion of myself and what I wanted to be paid, so I told Charlie I had to have a hundred dollars a week, which was practically unheard of then. He offered me sixty-five and tips, but I said no, so he said all right, a hundred, and he'd keep the tips. People threw a lot of money out on the floor after a show, and when we played for Ethel Waters and suchlike they'd come off with a bosomful of it. Charlie Johnson had a location band—Smalls' Paradise in Harlem in the winter and a similar place in Atlantic City in the summer. We had a lot of contests with visiting bands. We always won. I was doing all right with Charlie, but this is how I left: Ed Smalls, who owned the Paradise, adopted me. He was from Charleston, and all eighteen of his waiters were from Charleston. I was undependable, and I was late a lot for the show, which hit at nine o'clock. And it was two bits in the pot for the Christmas party every time you were late. So Ed Smalls told me to just get there by midnight and everything would be fine. The musicians didn't like anyone getting such special treatment, particularly a kid. Charlie called a meeting and said, 'You, Jabbo, bring yourself in at nine, or that's it.' The composer Con Conrad had been after me to join the band of 'Keep Shufflin',' which he was producing. So I quit Charlie

Johnon. Late in 1927, I had made a recording of 'Black and Tan Fantasy' with Duke Ellington, and Duke had asked me to go into the Cotton Club with him. He'd offered me ninety dollars, but by that time everybody claimed I was the best in New York and I was getting a hundred and fifty a week. I said no, and he hired Freddy Jenkins. The night before I recorded with Duke, somebody stole my horn. I had to go to a music store and get a replacement, and the mouthpiece was way too big. I had a hell of a time hitting that opening high C in my solo, but I made the session."

Light Everywhere

Richard Sudhalter, the cornettist, jazz reviewer, and biographer of Bix Beiderbecke, once mused over the trumpeter Adolphus (Doc) Cheatham: "The trumpet is an almost athletic instrument, and most trumpet players, through sheer fatigue, start to go off the rail in their sixties. So to hear a trumpeter that old play well is rare, but to hear Doc Cheatham, who's well into his seventies, play without any quaver or cutting back of tone or loss of clarity is truly exceptional. Of course, he rations himself. He takes short solos, and he never overblows, so when he has to he delivers. I used to see him at Mahogany Hall, in Boston, when I was a kid, and I remember the way he stood, just so: the arms out, the horn up, everything strong and right on the button—and, my Lord, that was in the early fifties. I think Joe Smith was the great light in his life as a trumpeter, and that's heartening— to see a man go not the way of Louis Armstrong but another way and succeed so beautifully for so long." Sudhalter was lucky to catch sight of Cheatham at all. Cheatham had begun the twenty or so years he spent as a lead trumpeter with Latin-American bands, and his occasional jazz appearances were generally limited to gigs with Wilbur De Paris's band, in which he played second trumpet to Sidney De Paris. In 1957, when he was chosen to appear on the CBS "Sound of Jazz" program with such trumpeters as Red Allen, Rex Stewart, Joe Wilder, Emmett Berry, Roy Eldridge, and Joe Newman, he refused to take any solos, agreeing only to play obbligatos behind Billie Holiday on her blues "Fine and Mellow." (That segment has become a classic, and so have Cheatham's exquisite background turnings.) Before the fifties, Cheatham had been a lead trumpeter with Sam Wooding and with Cab Calloway. He had also been part of Eddie Heywood's band, a small ensemble group built around its leader's Earl Hines piano. He was more audible in the sixties. He made a beautiful recording on the Prestige label with Shorty Baker, and he played no fewer than four solos on a Victor recording built around the rackety New Orleans alto saxophonist Cap'n John Handy. He also worked with Benny Goodman. In the last five years, he has become almost commonplace. At long last, he has made a couple of recordings of his own, and he has had extended engagements at Crawdaddy. He also turns up at Eddie Condon's and Sweet Basil and the West End Café and at various festivals here and abroad. All this exposure has strengthened him. Cheatham plays with more confidence and beauty now than he did when Sudhalter first heard him.

He belongs with those choice lyrical trumpeters who first came forward in the thirties and forties—Bill Coleman, Frankie Newton, Benny Carter, Joe Thomas, Buck Clayton, Shorty Baker, Emmett Berry, Harry Edison, Bobby Hackett, Charlie Shavers, Joe Wilder. Their idols were Louis Armstrong and Joe Smith and Roy Eldridge, and they have been distinguished by their originality and melodic grace, by their humor and poetic intensity. They like the middle register, their tones are handsome and range from Berry's rough querulousness to Hackett's and Wilder's luminosity, and they are almost all legato players. With the exception of

Shavers and Coleman, who are baroque players of the first order, these trumpeters favor spareness. Some are epigrammatic. Having grown up in the big bands (Lucky Millinder, Count Basie, Andy Kirk, McKinney's Cotton Pickers, Benny Carter, Duke Ellington), most of them prefer the roominess and acoustic ease of small groups. Their ranks have thinned. Newton, Baker, Hackett, Coleman, and Shavers are gone. Wilder works in Broadway pit bands, and Carter rarely plays trumpet anymore. Berry is retired, and Clayton and Thomas are semiretired. Only Edison and Cheatham—one in the West and the other in the East—keep the lamp of lyricism burning.

Cheatham lives in a four-room apartment in a small housing development on upper Lexington Avenue. The parlor is banked by a couple of blue settees and a small sideboard. It opens into a polished white kitchen, which contains a round table, with four chairs, and a big electric wall clock. The kitchen has a northeast window that slams like a cannon when the wind blows. A short hall leads to Cheatham's bedroom, where the pictures on the walls and the orderly clutter betoken the room of a kid who has just gone off to school, or of a bachelor, which Cheatham is most of the time. He is thin and snappy and patrician. He wears a trenchcoat and a cap, and sometimes he affects aviator glasses. His face is smooth and aquiline, and he has a tall, clear forehead. His frequent laugh is jumpy, and he speaks quickly, often repeating the final sentence of each paragraph. Recently, he sat in his kitchen and talked:

"My wife, Amanda, works for a family that lived on Park Avenue and moved to East Hampton. They wouldn't let her leave them, so she moved out there, and she comes in weekends. She's an Argentine, and I met her in the fifties when I was on tour with Perez Prado. I didn't think I'd get married again, but we have two children—a daughter and a son. I've always been a loner, and never much of a ladies' man. I married first in the thirties, when I got back from playing in Europe with Sam Wooding. It didn't last long. My second wife was a dancer at the Cotton Club. We were married seven years. I was with Cab Calloway then, and when I got sick and wasn't strong enough to play she'd harp on me: 'Why don't you get a job? Why don't you get a job?' I can't stand that. I'd rather be alone. She finally went home to Texas and married somebody else. I like being alone. I shop, I cook, I iron, I clean the house. I was taught how to do those things as a kid. That was in Nashville, where I was born in 1905. It was a pleasant place to grow up. My mother was named Alice Anthony, and she was from Atlanta. She taught school there and in Nashville, and later on she was a laboratory assistant. She was the kind of mother who's always in your corner. My older brother, Marshall, became a dentist. He was named after my father, who was from Cheatham County, Tennessee. I never knew much about his family. I do know that he was partly descended from the Choctaws and Cherokees who settled Cheatham County, and that he had a lot of brothers and sisters, one of them a teacher at Tuskegee Institute. His mother might have been white, perhaps English. My father was a barber, and he had travelled a lot, particularly on the Mississippi riverboats. He was a proud man who stood straight as an arrow. He had his own barbershop, right in the heart of the business district. In fact, he owned the whole building. That came about this way: he had helped a Mr. Mooney, an immigrant, start a candy concern, and Mooney had made a lot of money, so he bought a building for my father. The building had three stories. The barbershop, which had four chairs, was on the ground floor, and there was a tailor on the top floor, and baths on the second floor, so that when a gentleman came in he could have a shave and shine and cut, take a bath while his suit was pressed, and come out looking and feeling like a million dollars. My father worked seven days a week—on Sundays he shaved the sick, who couldn't get out. We had our own house, in a good neighborhood. It cost seven thousand dollars, and my father bought it through his friends. He also had a car, and sometimes I'd drive him to work, but he would never let me leave him off in front of the shop, because he thought it would look like he was putting on airs. He loved to walk, and we walked forever. And he loved to go to ballgames. Our team, in the old Negro leagues, was the Nashville Elite Giants.

"I started playing music when I was about fifteen. There was a little beatup church in our neighborhood called the Phillip's Chapel, and the deacon was an intelligent, stubby man named Meredith. He organized a band for kids, the Bright Future Stars. I started on drums, and he switched me to cornet. I practically taught myself. The only lessons I had were from two brothers, Professor N. C. Davis and Professor C. M. Davis. They came once a week and gave lessons for a quarter each. They'd been circus trumpeters, and they drank a lot. When one was too drunk, the other one came. You'd smell the whiskey on their breath. I don't remember hearing much of anything musically in Nashville in 1920. Radio was just coming in, and there wasn't much yet in the way of jazz recordings. But Paul Whiteman and Ted Lewis came through, and so did the blues singers. By 1923 or 1924, I was working in the pit band at the Bijou Theatre. A New Orleans trumpet player, George Jefferson, was in the band, and he was a lot of help. The rough element went to the Bijou, but I'd see the principal of the high school there, his face covered with a newspaper. I worked behind all the great blues singers—Mamie Smith and Bessie Smith and Clara Smith. Clara Smith was twice as powerful as Bessie. She shook the rafters. And she was rough. You better not make one mistake when she came off the train tired and mean and evil. Ethel Waters also came through. She brought Fletcher Henderson on piano and Joe Smith on cornet. Joe Smith wore white bell-bottoms, and when he played he'd stand with one foot on a hassock. He looked beautiful, and he sounded beautiful.

"I left Nashville the first time in 1925, and by 1926 I was in Chicago. I left with Marion Hardy's band, and when I got to Chicago I was with John Williams' Synco Jazzers. He married Mary Lou Williams around that time. My parents didn't care for my becoming a musician at all. I think they hoped I'd somehow study to be a doctor, because I used to play in a little band over at the Meharry Medical College—which is how I got my nickname. My father had seen enough drunken circus musicians, and he didn't want me to end up that way. So it hurt him very bad when I left home and went on the road. I spent a year in Chicago. I didn't have much luck, and I lost a lot of weight. The New Orleans musicians had everything wrapped up. But land-ladies were very sympathetic in those days, and six of us got a room together, and we managed to make it, with God's help. There was a little restaurant nearby called Poor Me, and I'd go get the food and we'd divide it up. I met Lil Armstrong, and I had some gigs with her, and Albert Wynn, the trombonist, put me in his band as a saxophonist. I'd taken up the saxophone about the same time as the cornet, and I played it just about as well. Once, Louis Armstrong asked Albert Wynn could I sit in for him with Erskine Tate at the Vendome Theatre. Louis had a feature number, 'Poor Little Rich Girl,' which I had played with Wynn. Louis was a sensation, and the Vendome was packed every night. I'll never forget how that audience screamed when I came onstage and how, when the spotlight caught me and the audience realized I wasn't Louis, they got quieter and quieter. I had memorized Louis's solo, and I played it note for note. I got nice applause, but the musicians in the band, they wouldn't talk to me—not one word. Later, Louis and I became very good friends.

"I heard a lot of music in Chicago. King Oliver had a soft band. The New Orleans style was very different. It was a sweet type of jazz—a melodic type of jazz. Oliver himself was very different from Joe Smith and Johnny Dunn, who were the best horn players I'd heard. He had a nice, quiet tone, and he knew what he was doing every minute. He used a lot of mutes—I picked up my mute technique from him—and he'd growl a little. Freddie Keppard reminded me of a military trumpeter playing jazz. He was very loud, and he didn't have any of Oliver's polish. One night, he blew a mute right out of his horn and across the dance floor, and it became the talk of Chicago. After that, everybody piled in night after night to see him do it again, but he never did. It was true about his fear of other musicians' stealing his stuff. I saw him put a handkerchief over his valves when he was playing, so that nobody could follow his fingering."

Listening to Doc Cheatham play is like looking at a Winslow Homer: there is light everywhere. Some of the light is reflected. Here is a Louis Armstrong connective phrase, a Buck Clayton vibrato, a Joe Smith sustained note, a Joe Thomas epigram. But Cheatham is a courteous, generous man, and perhaps these reflections are more in the nature of salutes—of nods thrown in the direction of people he admires. The elegance and lyricism and grace of his playing are his own, as is his sense of structure. His solos are flawlessly designed. Each phrase follows the last freshly and without hesitation. There is none of the disconnected brittleness or brassy striving that afflicts many jazz trumpeters. Presented to the listener in their glistening perfection, Cheatham's solos give the impression that they have been written, edited, and tested—when, of course, they have been instantly spun out of his head. The light in his improvisations brings up pure, soft colors, and the planes his solos are built of—planes that turn ceaselessly this way and that—are alizarin and taupe and ultramarine and viridian. There is no silver or gold, no black or white. Cheatham's tone is complete and jubilant. At first, his rhythmic sense seems old-fashioned. He has a staccato, elbowing attack. Each note clears away the silence before it. Each note is an announcement. But he is also a legato player, whose rests allow beats to slip by, and though he is invariably on time at the end of each solo, he is cool about how he has done it. He likes big intervals and sudden off-course phrases. He is a consummate muted player, and when he uses a plunger mute he can growl and muse and flutter and whisper with all the sly bravado of Cootie Williams. One of Cheatham's aunts told him when he was starting out, "Stand up straight when you play, throw out your chest, hold your arms horizontal, and keep your head back." And there he is: his arms winglike, his back concave, his trumpet pointed at the sky. It is a heraldic stance.

"I gave up on Chicago in 1927," Cheatham said, "and joined Bobby Lee's band at the Silver Slipper in Philadelphia. We played the Sea Girt Inn, in New Jersey, that summer, and in the fall I went back to Philly with Wilbur De Paris. He was a tight man. I lived at his house, and he charged me for rent and food—he kept a file on all the extra biscuits I ate. The later part of 1928, I went to New York, where I heard Jabbo Smith, who was faster than Louis and seemed even greater to me. I was with Chick Webb for a bit, and Sam Wooding grabbed me and I travelled around Europe three years in his band. I could read like a top by then, and I played lead trumpet while Tommy Ladnier handled the jazz solos. Ladnier was a moody man, a moody player, but he could go when he wanted to. We played nothing but first-class places, and it was very exciting to me. I rejoined Marion Hardy when I got back, then went to McKinney's Cotton Pickers. Joe Smith and Rex Stewart were in the band, and it was like a college of jazz. But one of the teachers wasn't in the band, and that was Bix Beiderbecke. All trumpet players had been playing alike when Bix came along a year or two before and opened the gate. He was doing things we had never heard. He was a lyrical player, but he was also staccato and bright. He had a speaking, *trumpet* way of playing. Anyway, the Cotton Pickers ran out of money, so somebody stole the band book and wouldn't give it back until everything was settled up. The Depression was beginning to hit the regional bands hard, and they were falling by the road. It wasn't until Benny Goodman made it in 1935 that people started going out again to hear the bands, and Benny did it in a *national* way for the first time. I had an offer to go with Cab Calloway at the Cotton Club in 1931, and I took it. I was with Cab eight years, and he

was the greatest leader I ever worked for. He ran around
with us, and he could be playful, and even rowdy, but you
had to be at work on the dot and you had to play right. Cab
had learned to read and he had a good ear. That band made
tables of money. They made so much more nights they'd
pack it in the drum case. I got a hundred dollars a week
every Friday like clockwork, and once I got paid twice and
was told to keep it.

"I've never been strong, and in 1939 I fell sick. I was run-
down and anemic, and they hospitalized me for nine weeks.
I guess it was being on the road so much and not eating and
resting properly. It certainly wasn't drink, because I have
never been a drinker. I discovered a long time ago that you
can't drink and play jazz well. You have to stay sober to
think fluently. Drunks tend to be cliché players. Of course,
you're not too popular when you don't drink. You're considered a sissy. They never did figure out what was wrong
with me, and I didn't regain my full strength, so that I could
play the way I really wanted to, until the sixties. It took that
long, and at one point a doctor told me, 'Doc, I don't know.
Maybe you better just lay down the rest of your life.'
When I got out of the hospital, I went to Europe for a few
months to rest. Then I joined Teddy Wilson's big band and
after that Benny Carter's, but I wasn't up to par. I quit playing and took a job in the post office. In 1943, I tried it again,
in Eddie Heywood's little group—which wasn't too hard,
because Eddie wrote everything out and took long piano
solos. It was around this time that I ran into my friend Juan
Tizol, who was with Duke Ellington, and he said, 'You
should be in the Ellington band. Come over to the theatre
in Brooklyn where we're working and I'll introduce you to
Duke.' Well, I have never asked anyone for a job. I couldn't
do it—on pride, and because it puts you in their power. But
I went. I went to Duke's dressing room and I sat there all
day—like a fool. Duke would change and do a show and
change again and do another show and change again, and
the whole time he never said a thing to me beyond 'How
you been?' and like that. And, of course, there were a lot

of people around. Duke always had his entourage. So finally I said, 'Nice seeing you, Duke. So long.' And we shook hands. That was it until seven or eight years ago, when his sister called me and asked me to join the band. But I'd had an operation, and I couldn't make it.

"I live with my horn. I practice every day—sometimes until ten o'clock at night. I listen to records of all my favorite players—Charlie Shavers and Sidney De Paris and Shorty Baker and Joe Thomas and Louis. Taking a solo is like an electric shock. First, I have no idea what I will play, but then something in my brain leads me to build very rapidly, and I start thinking real fast from note to note. I don't worry about chords, because I can hear the harmonic structure in the back of my mind. I have been through all that so many years it is second nature to me. I also have what I think of as a photograph of the melody running in my head. I realize quickly that there is no one way to go in a solo. It's like travelling from here to the Bronx—there are several ways, and you must choose the right way immediately. So I do, and at the same time I never forget to tell a story in my solo. I have always listened for that in other horn players, and it's the only way I know how to play. I'm not a high-note player generally, but sometimes the things I'm playing run me up there, and it frightens me a little. But I get down all right. I keep in shape by walking. Like my father. I'll walk down to Forty-second Street, go over to the musicians' union, on West Fifty-second Street, and walk home. I don't like getting back from work at three or four in the morning anymore. I like getting back early, so I can take my sitz bath and go to bed and be up at seven or eight. I love the morning, the morning air—the country air, which is what city air is like in the morning if you catch it quick enough. And I love a big breakfast, which doesn't taste the same later in the day. I'll make myself juice and oatmeal. Or I'll cook fried oysters that I get from a friend out in Jamaica. Or I'll have grits and some fish. Sometimes I'll have chicken or turkey, or sliced tomatoes and pancakes. I guess I'm kind of retired now. I get the Social Security, and I only work three or four nights a week—unless I get a month in Europe or a couple of weeks in Toronto. I got a standing ovation in Toronto a while ago, and that felt very good. It doesn't happen often in a lifetime, and it makes all the rough times worth it. I'm almost the last of the line. I've talked to kids who come to hear us who don't even know who Louis Armstrong is. But they listen. 'How do you do that?' they'll ask. 'That's beautiful,' they'll say. When I'm gone, it'll be just about over, my kind of playing. It will be as if it hadn't existed at all, as if all of us hadn't worked so long and hard."

Fats

Fats Waller got going early. He was born Thomas Wright Waller, in New York, on May 21, 1904. He was the seventh of eleven children, only five of whom survived. His parents, Edward Waller and Adeline Lockett, had moved from Virginia in 1888, when they were sixteen. Edward Waller was a successful carter, and, a self-cured stammerer, he became a preacher for the Abyssinian Baptist Church. Young Waller started at the harmonium and piano at six, and at fifteen he was playing the piano and organ at the Lincoln Theatre in Harlem, for twenty-three dollars a week. It was not a career his father favored. He was also hanging out with the pianists Willie the Lion Smith and James P. Johnson. Smith summed Waller up neatly in "Music on My Mind." "When we met, he wasn't born yet," Smith wrote. "He was wished on me. From that time on he followed the Lion and The Brute [Johnson] around. We both tutored him and I was the one who first told him to sing and make faces to draw attention. He was always mimicking West Indian talk; I could see where he was a natural as a showman. He had that magnetic personality with big brown eyes . . . He was shy at first and I would loosen him up with sauterne. Later he drank ABD's [anybody's drink] and started travelling so fast through life . . . he just never took the time to set himself in the right direction. When he jumped from the basement to five thousand dollars a week, I told him to slow down. 'Lion,' he would say, 'one never knows, do one!' "

In 1920, Waller's mother, whom he doted on, died, and he moved into a schoolmate's home. The next year, he married Edith Hatchett, and they had a son, Thomas, Jr. But Waller was either on the town or on the road, and they separated. (Waller was not designed for the diurnal life; during the next decade, Edith Waller had him sent to jail twice for failure to pay alimony.) By the time he was in his early twenties, he had met Count Basie and given him pointers on the organ, made his first records (piano solos: "Muscle Shoals Blues" and "Birmingham Blues"), written his first songs, and begun studying with Leopold Godowsky, the pianist and composer. Waller married Anita Rutherford in 1926, and they had two sons, Maurice and Ronald. In 1928, after working in Chicago with Louis Armstrong and Earl Hines, he wrote half the music for "Keep Shufflin'." He and James P. Johnson played double piano in the pit, and they made four numbers for Victor with Jabbo Smith on trumpet and Garvin Bushell on reeds. Waller was on pipe organ and Johnson on piano, and the music was a unique combination of the roaring and the delicate and the mercurial. Waller also wrote a revue called "Hot Chocolates" with Andy Razaf the next year, and, as was becoming his scandalous wont, sold the rights—to Irving Mills, for five hundred dollars. ("Ain't Misbehavin'" and "Black and Blue" were among the songs.) Waller first heard Art Tatum in 1931, was duly thunderstruck, and took off for Paris, where he played the "God-box" in Notre Dame. He weathered the early Depression with radio jobs (WLW in Cincinnati and WABC in New York), and in 1934 he made the first of four hundred or so small-band sides for Victor. The recordings put him squarely before the jazz public, and by 1938 Waller was probably as well known as Louis Armstrong. The two men were recorded that year on a radio show but, rather surprisingly, did not mix well. Waller's staccato high-register accompaniment gets in Armstrong's way, and Armstrong's longer melodic lines make Waller sound chunky. Armstrong loved Waller's *esprit,* but he never hired a stride pianist.

Waller's small-band records were hobbled by a fixed instrumentation (trumpet, tenor saxophone or clarinet, piano, guitar, bass, drums), second-class musicians (Herman Autrey, Bugs Hamilton, Eugene Sedric, Al Casey, Cedric Wallace, Slick Jones), the three-minute time limit, and often abysmal materials ("Florida Flo," "The Love Bug'll Bite You," "Us on a Bus"), but they were remarkably flexible and springy. The order of solos and vocals, who was to accompany whom, whether to use mutes or not—all were ceaselessly fiddled with. The success of the records depended on Waller, for he was never inaudible, and when he was on course (most of the time), they swung very hard. Waller's famous ad-libs seemed to spill right out of his records, and were addressed to his musicians or to the listener or to the subject of the song. These side-of-the-mouth utterances gave his records a kind of universality. He starts "Serenade for a Wealthy Widow" by saying, "Woman, they tell me you're flooded with currency. Well, come on—give, give, give!" On "How Can You Face Me," he urges a trombone soloist on with "Ah, you're a dirty dog, get out in the street, get out, get out! How can you face me now," which is followed by "No, I didn't go there last night. No, you know I wasn't there, either. I went to the other place." At the close of "Do Me a Favor," he talks very fast: "Listen, honey, have you got a dollar-ninety, cuz I got the dime? You might as well go out there and find the parson." And at the close of "Your Feet's Too Big" he says, "Your pedal extremities are really obnoxious." Perhaps his classic ad-lib came in the middle of a slow, lyrical version of "Sometimes I Feel Like a Motherless Child," done as an organ solo a few months before he died. Midway, Waller, who has been still, says, "I wonder what the poor people are doin' tonight. I'd love to be doin' it with 'em." At first, the remark seems to shatter the mood; then it seems both funny and wrenching.

Waller took his band all over the country between recording sessions, and in the late thirties or early forties Eudora Welty heard him and wrote a strange and indelible short story called "Powerhouse." The surface is expressionistic and slightly ominous. Powerhouse is playing a white dance in a small town in Mississippi, and just before intermission at midnight he tells his musicians that he has received a mysterious telegram from a Uranus Knockwood, saying "YOUR WIFE IS DEAD." Powerhouse talked to his wife on the telephone the night before, and she threatened to jump out the window. The rest of the story is taken up by Powerhouse's self-pitying and angry embellishments on the notion that his wife *has* done what she said. At first, the band members believe him, then they understand and go along with the fantasy: imagine the worst and you keep at bay the devil and all the "no-good pussyfooted crooning creepers" that hang around musicians. You also keep your ego intact. Being on the road in the black Southern night tries the soul, and humor is its balm. Eudora Welty's observations of Powerhouse/Waller are marvellous. Romanticism is a form of astonishment, and here is how she introduces him:

> There's no one in the world like him. You can't tell what he is. "Nigger man"?—he looks more Asiatic, monkey, Jewish, Babylonian, Peruvian, fanatic, devil. He has pale grey eyes, heavy lids, maybe horny like a lizard's, but big glowing eyes when they're open. He has African feet of the greatest size [Waller wore a fifteen shoe], stomping, both together, on each side of the pedals. He's not coal black—beverage colored—looks like a preacher when his mouth is shut, but then it opens—vast and obscene . . . He's in a trance; he's a person of joy . . . He listens as much as he performs, a look of hideous, powerful rapture on his face. Big arched eyebrows that never stop travelling . . . There he is with his great head, fat stomach, and little round piston legs, and long yellow-sectioned strong big fingers.

Powerhouse starts a tune:

His hands over the keys, he says sternly, "You-all ready? You-all ready to do some serious walking?"—waits—then, STAMP. Quiet. STAMP, for the second time . . . Then a set of rhythmic kicks against the floor to communicate the tempo. . . . O Lord! . . . hello and good-by, and . . . they are all down the first note like a waterfall.

Powerhouse sings:

On the sweet pieces such a leer for everybody! He looks down so benevolently upon all our faces and whispers the lyrics to us. . . . He's going up the keyboard with a few fingers in some very derogatory triplet-routine, he gets higher and higher, and then he looks over the end of the piano, as if over a cliff.

The band goes to a black beer joint during intermission, and the exchanges with the waitress are perfect. Powerhouse says, "Come here, living statue, and get all this big order of beer we fixing to give."

The waitress, setting the tray of beer down on a back table, comes up taut and apprehensive as a hen. "Says in the kitchen . . . that you is Mr. Powerhouse. . . ."

"They seeing right tonight, that is him," says Little Brother.

"You him?"

"That is him in the flesh," says Scoot.

"Does you wish to touch him?" asks Valentine. "Because he don't bite."

Duke Ellington knew that the only constant on the road is motion, and he often asked Harry Carney where they were going next. Powerhouse says to one of his musicians,

"What you tell me the name of this place?"

"White dance, week night, raining, Alligator, Mississippi, long ways from home."

"Uh-huh."

The musicians return to the stand after intermission:

He didn't strike the piano keys for pitch—he simply opened his mouth and gave falsetto howls—in A, D and so on . . . Then he took hold of the piano, as if he saw it for the first time in his life, and tested it for strength, hit it down in the bass, played an octave with his elbow . . . He sat down and played it for a few minutes with outrageous force, and got it under his power—a bass deep and coarse as a sea net—then produced something glimmering and fragile, and smiled. And who could ever remember any of the things he says? They are just inspired remarks that roll out of his mouth like smoke.

Waller's life was far less phantasmagoric. He had never cared for the road and its discomforts, physical and racial, and he frequently expressed amazement at how white audiences would cheer their heads off when he was on the stand and then send him across the tracks to spend the night. More and more, he quit engagements before they were over, or simply didn't turn up, pleading homesickness for Harlem, where he could be found a day or two later, cooling it at home or sitting in at the nearest club. Waller had become an alcoholic, and it was eroding his life. He was a master illusionist, who fooled everyone, including himself. He made a perpetual joke of his drinking (the late Eddie Condon, to say nothing of W. C. Fields, was also expert at this jiggery-pokery), and it became part of the furniture of his huge, comic, boisterous self: the ever-present bottle on or under the piano at recording dates and on the bandstand; the "liquid ham-and-eggs" he had for breakfast the moment he awoke; the multitude of drinks he had backstage at his Carnegie Hall concert, in 1942, which was a disaster. But Waller had a cavernous capacity, and his drinking rarely got in the way of his music. On his records, his playing and diction are invariably clean and clear. There is no evidence of uncertain time or of anything out of control.

Waller's comic spirit was ungovernable. He offered the rare gift of comic catharsis, and apparently it never failed him, onstage or off. He was always on, whether he was meeting for the first time a precocious piano player and singer named Bobby Short ("He marched right over, picked

me up in his arms, and hugged me. 'You could be my son,'
he said. 'You even look like me a little bit . . . Say, who's
your mother?' ") or sixteen-year-old Mary Lou Williams
("I played for him and he picked me up and threw me in
the air"). One can do the Freudian two-step with Waller,
but it isn't much help. Did he poke fun at everything because he was trying to offset the melancholy caused by his
mother's death and his father's obtuseness? Did he make people laugh to conceal his deep shyness? Did he laugh (and
drink) out of sheer terror at life? Joel Vance offers this
gloomy paragraph in "Fats Waller: His Life and Times":

> His attention span was that of a small boy: he wrote tunes
> as toys, forgetting them as quickly as they ceased to please
> him or to bring him quick money. He was constantly in
> search of adventures, but the adventures had to take place
> in comfortable and convivial surroundings—the company of
> his musical peers in Harlem, a backstage bash with cast and
> chorus girls, or a gargantuan eating session. Waller's high
> living was a succession of self-induced birthday parties. He
> never completed the emotional transition from childhood to
> maturity. At the price of preserving his childhood in alco-
> hol, he managed to let his creative powers flow to the
> fullest . . .

Whichever or whatever, Waller *was* a funny man, even
when he played the piano and kept his mouth shut. He was
the last of the great stride pianists, and he perfected the style.
Stride piano had grown out of the oompah bass and filigreed
right hand of ragtime. Its main concerns were rhythmic and
melodic: keep that rocking two-beat motion going, no matter how slow, and keep the melody uppermost, no matter
how strong the urge to embellish. It was a chordal way of
piano playing, both in the left hand, where tenths alternated
with seesawing chord-and-single-note figures (Waller's huge
hands spanned more than a tenth), and in the right, where
chords, often played staccato or against the beat, were
spelled by pearly, Lisztian runs. When Waller reached his
prime, in the early thirties, stride piano had been made to
seem old-fashioned by the brilliant inventions of Earl Hines,

who had put jazz piano playing on a four-four basis, straight-
ened out and added muscle to its arpeggios, substituted single-note melodic lines for the squat right-hand chords, and
added various punctuations to the left hand. Hines notwith-
standing, two great—and antithetical—pianists came out of
Waller: Count Basie and Art Tatum. Basie turned Waller's
style into ingenious musical telegraphy; he used two notes
for every twenty of Waller's, and got even stronger results.
Tatum was probably influenced by Waller harmonically
and pianistically, but the only time he openly bowed in his
direction was at breakneck tempos, when he used an unbe-
lievably fast oompah bass that was both affectionate and
needling. (In 1938, when Tatum dropped in to hear Waller
at a club on Fifty-second Street, Waller introduced him by
saying, "I just play the piano, but God is in the house tonight.") Waller's pianistic humor was both sheer exuberance
and an inability to let foolishness be. He would use right-
hand trills and tremolos and high, bouncing offbeat figures
(pianistic falsetto) and, in his left hand, booms, and even an
occasional boogie-woogie bass—a form he said he despised.
When the material he had to record was particularly maudlin
(it is not clear whether Victor's A. & R. men thought it
would make hits or were slyly feeding it to Waller to see
how fine he would grind it), he gave it the rhapsody treatment, using lots of loud pedal and low, theatrical single
notes that summoned up Eddy Duchin. Waller was a superb
pianist. His touch was firm and clear, he rarely missed notes,
and he had a nice sense of dynamics. His time was metro-
nomic yet had the infinitesimal looseness that is part of
swinging. Waller loved the organ. It gave him room for
subtleties not possible on the piano and for his histrionic
tendencies. (Vance quotes Eugene Sedric as saying that
Waller often told him that "someday he might become a
preacher and go out and give sermons with a big band behind him.") He could moon and whisper and make bird and
wind and wave sounds; he could disport himself without
saying a word. He was the first jazz organist—which doesn't
mean much, since there have been few creditable jazz or-

ganists, and certainly none who have played the instrument
with his delicacy and attentiveness, Count Basie and Joe
Mooney excepted. But there was a weakness in Waller's in-
strumental attack: he had little feeling for the blues. His
rare blues excursions are glancing and breezy, and there isn't
much emotion. This peculiar lack afflicted all the stride
pianists as well as such Eastern pianists as Hines, Tatum, and
Erroll Garner.

Waller's endless vocal effects—mock-English and West
Indian accents, Bronx cheers, heavy aeolian sighs, parlando,
rubbery staccato diction—have been duly celebrated, but it
should be said that he was a first-rate singer. He had an excellent light baritone, faultless diction (when he chose), and
perfect intonation. Once in a while, he would sing a song
almost straight, and the slightly delayed rhythmic attack
and occasional embellishments revealed his respect for Louis
Armstrong, part of whose vocal on a 1932 "When It's Sleepy
Time Down South" Waller copies or parodies on the final
bridge of "Breakin' the Ice." Waller the songwriter was a
third and inseparable self. He wrote his songs quickly, and
they are notable on several counts: their very melodies
swing, they often resemble ragtime, and they are extremely
catchy. But the catchiness of "Ain't Misbehavin'" and "Jitter-
bug Waltz" is dangerous, for, as Alec Wilder has pointed
out, the "Beer Barrel Polka" is similarly attractive. Wilder
continued, "I don't think Waller had great melodic sensibil-
ity. I don't think he knew how to write long melodic lines.
Jerome Kern would have told him how, but I doubt that
Waller knew such an area of popular music. His melodic
lines are all made up of little pieces, of imitations. Each
phrase is sustained by an imitation, or partial imitation, of
the previous phrase. In a sense, he wrote like a barroom
piano player. His songs are often like the little glistening
phrases that good barroom piano players come up with. He
was the opposite of a pianist like Cy Walter. Walter didn't
like to improvise, and he didn't like jazz. But when he wrote
a song, it had a long and often complex melodic line. Waller
was a Tin Pan Alley writer. He wrote for fun. His songs

fell right in. They were written for the counter, for immediate sale. Give them to the band, give them to the singer. His songs were very different from, say, 'You Go to My Head,' a complicated and beautiful song that astonishingly became a hit, or from 'Star Dust,' which is even harder to sing than 'The Star-Spangled Banner.' The intensity and brilliance squeezed into such songs escaped Waller completely. But his songs make you think of him, of his playing, of his joy of living, and there's certainly nothing wrong with that."

By the early forties Waller was making very good money. But he was still casting about. Was he basically a comedian, a bandleader, a songwriter, or a jazz musician? He recorded on organ and celeste behind Lee Wiley (he was a superb accompanist on both piano and organ), and he gave his depressing Carnegie Hall concert. He wrote the music for "Early to Bed," which had a decent run on Broadway and was the first non-black musical written by a black. He filmed "Stormy Weather," with Bill Robinson and Lena Horne, and he appeared on the radio with Edgar Bergen and Charlie McCarthy. He was on the verge of going national. He went on the soft-drink wagon for a year, then switched to sauterne. But his massive appetite had weakened, and so had his resistance. Late in 1943, he worked the Zanzibar Room in Los Angeles and caught a bad cold. He took ten days off and couldn't completely shake it, but finished the job. He entrained for New York, telling his manager Ed Kirkeby that he was exhausted. He slept an entire day and night, and died in his sleep of bronchial pneumonia just as the train pulled into Kansas City.

Deathbed utterances are immutable, but misinterpretations aren't. Kirkeby reported in his "Ain't Misbehavin' ' ":

> About two [the morning of Waller's death] I opened the door to the sleeper and was hit by a blast of cold air.
> "Jesus, it's cold in here!" I said, as I saw Fats was awake.
> "Yeah, Hawkins is sure blowin' out there tonight," Fats replied.

> The train was roaring through the Kansas plains in a
> howling blizzard, which reminded Fats of the blustery sax
> playing of his friend Coleman Hawkins.

Both Vance and Maurice Waller repeat Kirkeby's poetic allu-
sion, but that is surely not what Waller meant. A "hawkins"
in the old black argot is snow or ice or a cold wind.

Opinions about the light and joy and kindness that Waller
shed wherever he went are unanimous. Pee Wee Russell told
the jazz scholar Jeff Atterton of the last time he saw Waller: "My wife and I were walking along a Village street
and we passed the Greenwich Village Inn . . . Fats Waller's name was out front. Fats Waller appearing and so on.
We went in for a quiet drink or what I hoped would be a
quiet drink. We found ourselves at a ringside table. Fats
was on. He sat in the middle of the dance floor at a small
piano with the spotlight on him. And it took him a tenth
of a second to see me. He greeted me as though we were
meeting any place else but from opposite sides in a night
club and then refused to play unless I played with him. One
of the men in [his] . . . band loaned me his clarinet and
Fats and I had a very private party. We . . . played the
blues. The customers may not have liked it but I had a hell
of a time." The Cape Cod pianist Marie Marcus came to
New York from Boston to do a radio show in 1932, when
she was eighteen. Her experience had been limited to Boston
radio shows and to playing for a week at a Chinese restaurant called the Mahjong. "Tillie's Kitchen, in Harlem, was a
fried-chicken place," she has said, "and Bob Howard, who
sounded just like Fats Waller, was on piano. We went up
there quite often, and one night Fats himself came in. I remember the whole room lighted up. He played, and then
Howard persuaded me to play, even though I was scared to
death. Fats listened, and when I'd finished, he pointed to his
heart, and said, 'For a white gal, you sure got it there.' We
got to talking, and I told him that I would like to further
my education in jazz, and did he know a good teacher? He
looked at me and said, 'How about me?' I thought he was
putting me on, but he wasn't. He had a small office, with

two pianos, in the Brill Building, at 1619 Broadway, and during the next year or so, when he wasn't on the road or making records, he'd call me up and say, 'Come on down and let's play some piano.' You couldn't exactly call them lessons. We'd play duets, and then he'd play, and have me listen carefully to the things he did. He was very serious when we were working together, and I was grateful for every minute. He'd tell me, 'When you're playing jazz, remember the rhythm, remember the rhythm. Make the number of notes count. Tell a story, and get that feeling across to the people. Please the people by making it come from here.' "

Easier Than Working

Here is how the pianist Dick Wellstood made his living in the first half of 1978. He is referring to a daybook in which he records all his jobs: "On the third and fourth of January, I had a record date with Marty Grosz for the Aviva label, and on the fifth and sixth a Fats Waller date for Chiaroscuro. I played a private party on the ninth in Toms River, New Jersey. There was a remake of some of the Waller sides on the twelfth, because one of the participants had been under the weather the first time around. On the thirteenth, I did a party in Fairfield, Connecticut, and the day after that I went to Europe for six weeks, and gave concerts in Holland, Germany, Switzerland, Scotland, and England. I returned March 1st, and on the ninth did a concert at the Downtown Athletic Club. Four days later, I played a dance at the Harbor Island Spa, in West Long Branch, New Jersey, with my old friend Paul Hoffman, who leads a society band and has kept me alive off and on the last ten years. In fact, I had a regular job with Hoffman all during this time, and I would take a night or two off when extra dates came along. On the seventeenth, I had a solo appearance at the Bay Head Yacht Club, in New Jersey, and on the eighteenth a concert in Boston for George Wein. On the nineteenth, I did a duo with Kenny Davern in Morristown. Back to the Bay Head Yacht Club on the twenty-fourth for a solo appearance, and on the thirty-first for a duo. From the fourth to the ninth of April, Kenny Davern and I played the King of France Tavern, in Annapolis, and on the fourteenth and then on the nineteenth I was at the Yacht Club again. On the sixteenth, I took a band I'd had at Michael's Pub into the east branch of the Monmouth County Library, and on the twenty-second I sat in with a local Dixieland band at the Essex Fells Country Club. I did a two-day jazz party with Lou Stein at the Greenwich Country Club over the last weekend in April, and on May 5th I was back at the Yacht Club. I did a private recital in Toms River on the eighth. On the twelfth, thirteenth, nineteenth, and twenty-sixth, I was at the Yacht Club. On the twenty-eighth, Kenny Davern and I did another duo, at the Marriott Inn in Providence, and on June 2nd I was at the Yacht Club. On the third and fourth, I went with the World's Greatest Jazz Band to Andover, Massachusetts, and to Providence, and I sat in with a pickup group at a party in Summit on the ninth. I had a private party in Westport the eleventh, the Yacht Club on the sixteenth, and a wedding and the Yacht Club on the seventeenth. On the twenty-third, I did a private party in Chicago, and on the twenty-fifth a concert for the Newport Jazz Festival, in Stanhope, New Jersey. The Yacht Club closed June, and a party at Bill Buckley's home in Connecticut opened July. I might add that playing cha-chas with Paul Hoffman was just as much fun as anything I did in Europe. I have a fantastic weakness for workaday music like Hoffman's."

Here is how Wellstood made his living one night a year later. It was an evening in the middle of a long engagement at Eddie Condon's, on West Fifty-fourth Street. Wellstood, however, was not playing with the house band, or even as

the intermission pianist. As an experiment, he had been put
in the cocktail slot, from five-thirty to eight-thirty, and he
felt disoriented. The newspapers had listed him as the intermission pianist, and he suspected that his audience was
made up largely of neighborhood people, who talked sports
at the bar and gave him dirty looks when he began to play.
Wellstood arrived close to five-thirty, and the place—long
and narrow and high-ceilinged, with the bar and the bandstand on one side and banquettes and tables on the other—
was almost empty. Wellstood looked as if he had just come
in from judging an afternoon of racing at the Bay Head
Yacht Club. He had on pressed khakis, a white open-collared
shirt, and a blue blazer. His hair was tousled, and he wore
glasses that were halfway down his nose. He looked a lot
better than he had a year and a half before at an engagement
at the Carlyle. Then he had worn a tuxedo and a ruffled
shirt, which seemed to get between him and the keyboard,
and his hair had been forced into a pageboy. Later, he had
reported, "Opening night at the Carlyle was one of the
worst nights of my life. I couldn't play anything. My hands
had turned to lead and so had my head. Worst of all, Alec
Wilder had come in with a couple of friends, and I think it
was the first time he'd ever heard me live. He left immediately after the first set, looking pained in the brow, and that
made me feel terrible." At Condon's, Wellstood's attractive
beamish smile was back. He went to the bar and poured
himself a Coca-Cola, and sat down at a table. Laminated on
the tabletop was an enlarged facsimile of the Okeh label of
McKenzie and Condon's "Sugar," recorded in 1927, the
year Wellstood was born. He went to work on his hands.
He kneaded them, then made vigorous washing motions.
He pulled each finger, bent it backward and forward, and
pulled it again. He put the tips of his fingers together and
pressed them until his hands were palm to palm. He made
a fist of one hand and biffed the palm of the other, as if
he were breaking in a baseball mitt. Then he let both hands
hang loosely at his sides and shook them vigorously.
"Last evening wasn't bad at all," he said as he worked on

his hands. "I played well, and somewhere around eight a whole bunch of jazz fans came in, so I played for them until after nine. The only trouble was that the hammer of the G above middle C broke, but I doubt whether anybody noticed. Once, the English pianist Harold Bauer gave a concert in San Francisco, and an F-sharp got stuck just after he'd begun his last piece. He struggled with the note, trying to disguise that from the audience, trying to keep it from ruining the piece, trying to get *through*. When he came offstage, his manager said to him, 'Harold, I've listened to you up and down the world for twenty years, and that last piece was the most moving performance I have ever heard.' Which means that audiences are rarely on the same wavelength as performers. In fact, two very different things are going on at once. The musician is wondering how to get from the second eight bars into the bridge, and the audience is in pursuit of emotional energy. The musician is struggling, and the audience is making up dreamlike opinions about the music that may have nothing at all to do with what the musician is thinking or doing musically. If audiences knew what humdrum, daylight things most musicians think when they play, they'd probably never come."

He settled himself at the piano, a Baldwin grand that faces the door, and made mock pounding motions on the broken G. The bandstand at Condon's is roughly the size and shape of a longboat and contains a jumble of stools, chairs, tulip-shaped floor ashtrays, microphones, wires, and drums. The piano forms the cabin, and under it that evening was a large cardboard box of pretzels. Next to the pretzels were several tiers of shelves on which were salt and pepper, sugar, A.1., ketchup, cruets, and mugs, and beyond the piano's foreleg was a pail, and in it, for sweeping the deck, a broom. Wellstood went into a rollicking medium-tempo "There's a Small Hotel." He kept the lid of the piano shut. He had said that the piano, which he and the pianist John Bunch had been asked to choose, had a "glassy" sound. "Hotel" gave way to "Ain't Misbehavin'," which he has probably played eight thousand times, and into which he folded two more Wallers—"Squeeze Me" and "Blue Turning Gray Over You." Wellstood is more than a superb eclectic. He has been through and come out the other side of the music and styles of Scott Joplin, Joe Lamb, James P. Johnson, Willie the Lion Smith, Fats Waller, Zez Confrey, Earl Hines, Joe Sullivan, Count Basie, Cedar Walton, Ray Charles, Bill Evans, and Thelonious Monk. He has peered into their musical minds and savored the contents. He can play James P.'s "Carolina Shout" as Johnson played it, but you'd never mistake his version for Johnson's. Wellstood's touch is heavier, and he plays with more force. His rhythms and dynamic sense are more pronounced. He has removed the gingerbread from Johnson's playing, the airborne laciness, and replaced it with a sleek muscularity. In many ways, his Waller is better than Waller himself: he doesn't loaf the way Waller did, and he uses harmonic colorations Waller never thought of. Wellstood's blues are big, leisurely houses, full of tremolos, stark bass chords, and the sly humor of interpolation and retards. He has described stride piano this way: "Technically, stride piano is late Eastern ragtime. It's the way black pianists played in Harlem in the teens and twenties. It has an oompah bass—that is, your left hand makes a seesawing motion between a single bass note, struck at the bottom of the keyboard, and a chord struck some two and a half octaves farther north. The ragtime players only stretched an octave or an octave and a half, but the wider span gives you a fuller sound. The syncopated figures in the right hand include thirds and sixths, chromatic runs, and tremolo octaves. The left hand is the timekeeper—the keeper of momentum—and the right hand must never get too strong or it will make the left hand wag, and all the tension will go out of your playing. To me, James P. Johnson was the greatest stride pianist, and he was king until Art Tatum arrived in New York in the early thirties. James P. never forgave the pianist Joe Turner for first bringing Tatum here."

Wellstood slipped into a slow ballad—a form he more or less ignored until 1974, when he became a full-time solo pianist—and converted it into dense chordal layers, each rising slightly above the last, each filling the melodic confines. He moved on to Kurt Weill's "Barbara Song," and then to an Ellington medley, into which he fed bits of "Lush Life," "Sophisticated Lady," "Perdido," and "Caravan." He is an intense performer. His glasses make a nose-length slide every number, and every eight bars or so he gasps slightly. When he tries something he's not sure of, he purses his lips. If he blows it, he rattles his head and balloons his cheeks. Michel Legrand's "What Are You Doing the Rest of Your Life?" came next, and Wellstood went into a medium "How About You." Before that was done, he had applied James P. Johnson offbeat chords in the right hand, doubled the tempo for a ninety-mile-an-hour Art Tatum stride passage, let loose a few turn-around-and-jump Thelonious Monk runs, and demonstrated that it is a song he cares about. He closed the set with quiet readings of "She's Funny That Way," "I Concentrate on You," and "I Would Do Most Anything for You."

Wellstood got another Coca-Cola and sat down facing the door. Musicians spend most of their time in night clubs looking at the front door, for through it all blessings flow—audiences, money, girls, liquor, bookers, writers, and rich people looking for talent for their parties. Two men who had just come in and were standing at the bar approached, and one had a violin case. A Lord-this-cat-wants-to-sit-in look flickered across Wellstood's face, and his shoulders tightened. The man with the case said he'd come to fix the broken G, and he opened the case and took out his tools. Wellstood's shoulders relaxed, and he got up to show the tuner the damaged note.

Wellstood returned to his chair, and said, "I've been playing solo piano long enough to find out it can be very dangerous. Of course, it's wonderful in that you can do anything. You can play in any key, change keys when you want, halve the tempo, double it, triple it, play out of time, drop beats and pick them up later, accelerate or decelerate, finish a tune before the chorus ends. But you have to be damned sure that your time, which you play such hob with, doesn't go to hell and you find yourself speeding up or slowing down without premeditation. That's happened to some very good solo piano players. I'm one of those players who rely on the vessel of divine spirit—on what some call inspiration. When it comes by itself, you don't have to worry. You go into a trancelike state. But when it doesn't come you have to fall back on all kinds of patterns and figures. After all, when you're paid to play you *have* to play, and you can't go below a certain professional level. When I improvise, I think in terms of sounds, not of chords or melody. Some of my things may not have conventional harmonic continuity, but if they *sound* right and have rhythmic coherence, I'll do them. I learned to play the piano in public, and I've recently begun to try and relate my playing more to that public, even though it rarely grasps all that you're trying to do. At one time, I related my playing to the critics or to such eternal matters as the year that I first used an augmented ninth, or the year that I first played with Coleman Hawkins, or the like. For a long time, I had most of my playing mapped out. I liked the idea that once you got a solo worked up on a tune, you could use it over and over. After all, there are very few geniuses in jazz who create new things night after night. Most of us are lucky to have a couple of good, sparking nights a month. I think of myself as a contemporary musician who uses tools that are out of fashion. But lately I've been trying to get away from stride into more modern things, and when I do, I sound like Monk, which isn't so strange when you consider that Monk came directly out of the stride tradition. I like doing ballads and wandering around through a lot of new chords. I'm getting better as I get older, I think. My brain used to short-circuit a lot, but that's stopped. Actually, I've become quite excellent, and I often wonder why I don't work constantly."

The tuner told Wellstood that he had glued the hammer

and that it should be perfect by the time the house band started that night. Wellstood tilted back slightly in his chair and clasped his hands behind his head. He removed one hand, pushed his glasses up his nose, and clasped his hands again. He looked as if he were sitting in his East Side apartment, which is small and is lined with Smollett, Aldous Huxley, Robert Musil, Samuel Johnson, Nabokov, Meredith, Hazlitt, Gibbon, Chesterton, F. R. Leavis, and Thomas Love Peacock.

"Whenever I ask myself why I stay in this business, the answer is always the same: it's easier than working. I've tried writing. I can make a sentence, but my paragraphing is terrible. Anyway, if I had it for writing, I'd have written something important. I did try the law in the fifties. I read the Holmes-Laski correspondence, which I loved. It made me think, Why not go to law school? I did three years of prelaw at N.Y.U. in two years, and three years of law school at the New York Law School in two more years, and I passed my New York State bar exams. I was finishing work at three-thirty in the morning and getting up at eight for four years. I applied to about two hundred firms, and the closest I got to success was with a partner in a fancy place who knew something about jazz. That cheered me so much I told him a couple of ribald musician stories and that was that. When I was at N.Y.U., I studied a lot of Latin, which I really like. Now I'm about to start German so I can read Nietzsche, who makes me laugh.

"I joined Roy Eldridge about the time that I began prelaw. I was with Conrad Janis for seven years after Roy, and everybody passed through his band—Herman Autrey and Johnny Windhurst, Eddie Barefield, Art Trappier, Lawrence Brown, Dicky Wells. I worked on and off at the Metropole, at Seventh Avenue and Forty-eighth, from 1957 to 1965. All the musicians groused about it at the time, but, as John Bunch said the other day, 'that was it, that is where it was at.' I loved the energy and vulgarity of the place. It had a big marquee, and there were always winos dancing under it. The room was long and narrow, with mirrors going down both walls. A bar ran along almost the whole

north wall, and the musicians were obliged to stand in a
row on a platform above it. You couldn't hear yourself or
anyone else, and you played together by watching each
other in the mirrors. There was also a room upstairs for the
posh acts. Sometimes I'd be there all afternoon with a trio
and all night with someone like Red Allen. Between sets,
everybody went to the Copper Rail, across Seventh Avenue. It was just a plain bar, but hundreds of musicians
passed through every week. Honi Coles and the other tap-
dancers hung out and danced every night. Red Allen would
come over and bait Roy Eldridge, who always seemed to be
there, and Roy would get mad and take out his horn and
start demonstrating some musical point. The place became
a Mecca for European jazz fans, who'd stand around and
gawk at Roy and Ben Webster and Coleman Hawkins and
Charlie Shavers. At the time, I lived at Ninetieth and Lexington, and I'd pedal to work on my bike every afternoon.
I'd carry the bike up to the third floor to a little room where
I changed. After the afternoon session, I'd go back up and
put on a tux, and when I'd finished for the night, I'd put on
my street clothes and lug the bike down to the street, saying 'Pardon, pardon, pardon' to all the swells waiting on the
stairs to get in to see Chico Hamilton. I also spent time at
Nick's and Bourbon Street, and I was with Gene Krupa's
quartet for three years. Charlie Ventura was the horn player,
and it was a no-ego assignment. He was there to fill in between drum solos. Sometimes Krupa would let him go on
for chorus after chorus and sometimes he'd give him just
one. I liked Gene. He was a man who liked baseball and
church, and he got a good sound out of his drums. But with
that heavy bass drum and that on-the-beat playing, his head
was always back in the Chicago of 1928. I moved to Brielle,
New Jersey, in 1966, and by 1970 things were rough. Rock
had taken hold, and sometimes I didn't get a call for three
or four months at a time. It was then that I began working
with Paul Hoffman. I had to play floor shows as well as
cha-chas, and I loved it. It was the first time I ever felt use-
ful in the music business."
Wellstood smiled, looked at his watch, and returned to

the piano. He went immediately into Jelly Roll Morton's mournful "Sweet Substitute." James P. Johnson's rolling "Mule Walk" was followed by his "Caprice Rag," and Wellstood settled into a long "Everything I Have Is Yours." His public prose efforts have been limited largely to liner notes—generally written for his own albums, but not always. Here are two paragraphs from a set done for an Earl Hines album, in which Wellstood first kocks the Master down and then graciously picks him up and sends him on his way:

> Democratic Transcendent, his twitchy, spitting style uses every cheesy trick in the piano-bar catalog to create moving cathedrals, masterpieces of change, great trains of tension and relaxation, multidimensional solos that often seem to be *about* themselves or about other solos—"See, *here* I might have played some boogie-woogie, or put this accent *there*, or this run here, that chord there . . . or maybe a little stride for you beautiful people in the audience. . . ." Earl Hines, Your Musical Host, serving up the hot sauce.
>
> Hines is not a "stride" pianist. His rhythm is too straight four-four, too free. He does not possess the magisterial dignity of James P. Johnson, the aristocratic detachment of Art Tatum, the patience of Donald Lambert, the phlegmatic unflappability necessary to maintain the momentum of stride. Hines needs silence in the bass, room to let the flowers grow, space to unroll his showers of broken runs containing (miraculously) the melody within, his grace-noted octaves . . . and his wandering, Irish endings.

His prose often has a fine straight-from-the-shoulder turn. This is how he ends a long, complex description of stride piano playing, done as part of the liner notes to a Donald Lambert album:

> If all this sounds rather difficult and complicated, you may be sure that it is. In a world full of pianists who can rattle off fast omm-pahs or Chick Corea solo transcriptions or the Elliott Carter Sonata, there are perhaps only a dozen who can play stride convincingly at any length and with the proper energy.

"Everything I Have Is Yours" gave way to a cathedral of his own—a pondering, exultant "St. James Infirmary Blues," full of low-register turnings, broken tremolos, descending thirds, and ringing upper-register chords. Its flags moved in slow motion, and its final bass notes boomed. A snappy "If Dreams Come True," with a double-timed Art Tatum stride passage, went by, and then came a dreaming "Lullaby of Birdland," in which Wellstood kept turning the melody inward. He closed the set with Wayne Shorter's "Lester Left Town."

Wellstood went over to Seventh Avenue and had a hamburger, and when he got back he said, "Well, one more quick set should do it, considering how long I played last night. But first I'll rest a little. You need more rest at fifty than at forty, I've discovered. When people hear that I was born in Greenwich, they automatically think Hotchkiss, Yale, white shoes, and all the rest, but I was born in clam-digging Greenwich, not backcountry Greenwich. I was an only child. My father was in real estate, but he died when I was three. My mother made sixty dollars a month as a church organist, and we ate meat once a week. She also rented the other half of our house and gave two-dollar piano lessons. When things got too tight, she boarded me out in Maine, where she had friends. She was a short, determined lady, who was born in 1887. She graduated from Juilliard in 1911, before it was Juilliard, and she learned a lot of heavy Brahms there. I was born late in her life, so I grew up with people who were often a lot older, and that must be why I've spent so much time playing older music with older musicians. In many ways, I had a Victorian upbringing. My mother and I didn't get on too well, and I've figured out since her death that I probably *was* right about a lot of things we fought about. Anyway, I've completed the Victorian Age and am moving into the Edwardian. I went to public schools in Greenwich and in Maine, and for five years I went on scholarship to the Wooster School, in Danbury. I graduated in 1945. I wasn't an athletic star, and I found that people would pay attention to me if I played boogie-woogie after lunch at school, and it's all grown from that. By 1944, I was playing in a teen-age canteen in the cellar of the Greenwich Y. Charlie Traeger, who had taken up bass, heard me and invited me to a jam session at his house in Cos Cob. By the next year, I was jamming once a week in somebody's living room with Eddie Phyfe and Eddie Hubble and Johnny Glasel and Bob Wilber. I heard James P. Johnson and Willie the Lion Smith at the Pied Piper, on Barrow Street, in the summer of 1944, and they made a tremendous impression. I also heard a stride pianist named Johnny Williams, who played at the old Rye Hotel with a drummer who used temple blocks and had a picture painted on the front of his bass drum. Around then, we started going to the Hollywood Café, at a Hundred and Thirty-third and Seventh Avenue. It was owned by Tom Tillingham, but everyone called it Tom Tillum's. It was a regular nothing bar where the locals drank beer and yelled, but it had a back room with a red piano in it, and on Monday nights all the piano players gathered there—Art Tatum and Marlowe Morris and Willie Gant and the Beetle and Donald Lambert and Gimpy Irvis. Gimpy would take off his shoe and play the bass note with his left foot. In those days, musicians weren't as polite as they are now—'Hey, Dick, you sounded great!' 'Hey, Dick, you were really cooking!'—and they told each other how awful they thought they were. This was particularly true when they had cutting contests. One Monday, Donald Lambert sat down and played this fantastic stride piano. His left hand was a streak, his right hand a flea. Tatum was there with Marlowe Morris, who was one of the most interesting of the new pianists. Tatum didn't move after Lambert finished, and when the room quieted down, he leaned over to Morris and said, 'Take him, Marlowe,' and he did. I even sat in one night— right after Tatum. It was part gall and part stupidity. I was under the sway of moldy-fig writers who said that Tatum wasn't all that much, that James P. was still king. Anyway, we stopped going to Tillum's when singers started coming in eighteen in a row and doing 'Prisoner of Love' like Billy Eckstine. I saw a lot of James P. and Willie the Lion. James P. never said anything, and I was so in awe I never spoke to him. But I got to know Willie a little. Willie always said he was at least part Jewish—I heard him sing 'Alexander's Ragtime Band' in Yiddish, or what he claimed was Yiddish. He taught me his 'Zig-Zag,' which I made the mistake of learning by rote and consequently forgot completely.

"In 1946, Wilber and I moved into an apartment at Broadway and a Hundred and Eleventh. We'd do the Sunday-afternoon jam sessions at Jimmy Ryan's, and every now and then we'd go a couple of days without eating. I worked with Wilber and the old drummer Kaiser Marshall at the Savoy in Boston, and in 1948 Sidney Bechet sent for me to come and play at Jazz Limited in Chicago. I took it as the same sort of imperial summons as the one issued in 1922 by Joe Oliver from Chicago to Louis Armstrong in New Orleans. I went back to Boston with Wilber, and when Jimmy Archey took over the band, I stayed on. They had a businesslike attitude toward their work. They went to work on time, and they wore blue suits and white shirts and red ties, and they all knew how to read and were proud of it. They were cheerful and accomplished, and it was a job like any job, only it was night work instead of day work. Also, when they got a solo down on a certain tune, they played that solo, or something close to it, every time they did the tune. As a matter of fact, most jazz musicians repeat themselves all their lives, and have a good time doing it. It made me realize that maybe 'jazz' was largely the invention of a bunch of European-oriented intellectuals in the thirties—guys who thought they had found in 'jazz' a European-type art music."

During his final set, Wellstood played James P. Johnson, Gershwin, Zez Confrey, Cole Porter, Fats Waller, a rag, Maceo Pinkard, Eubie Blake, the Beatles, and Thelonious Monk. When he finished, an attractive blond-haired woman about Wellstood's age got up from a table near the door, and he said hello. He took her arm, and they went out, turning right instead of left, which would have taken them into the sunset.

Three Tones

Early one morning in the summer of 1967, when Duke Ellington had finished work at the Rainbow Grill and was having a steak at Jilly's with a group of friends, he was asked why he had never hired the great trombonist Vic Dickenson. It was evidently not a question he wished to answer directly, so he repeated the trombonist's name twice and added his own question: "Does he still have his three tones?" Ellington rarely put down exceptional musicians who hadn't passed through his academy, and what he probably meant was: Does Vic Dickenson still play as simply and beautifully as ever? The answer then was yes, and the answer now is still yes.

In the forty years since Dickenson quit travelling with big bands, he has been almost constantly on view in New York, and he has invariably worked and recorded with the champions, among them Sidney Bechet, Frankie Newton, Ben Webster, Sid Catlett, Buck Clayton, Edmond Hall, Red

Allen, James P. Johnson, Pee Wee Russell, Coleman Hawkins, Ruby Braff, and Bobby Hackett. Dickenson's presence
brightens every band he plays with. He is tall and thin, and
he has a long, wry, Lincoln face. His eyes are generously
lidded. He has a medium-sized, middle-register voice of a
kind that winds between other voices in a gathering. He is
a slow, laconic talker, and his laugh is concentrated and nasal. He is a calm, cool, funny man who wishes no offense to
life and hopes life will return his sentiments. In recent
years, he has preferred to sit down with his legs crossed
when he plays; he leans slightly to his left and balances himself by pointing his trombone to the right. When he heads
his own group, he pauses a long time between numbers and
shuffles through a pile of plastic-covered three-by-five cards
on which are typed the names of some three hundred songs.
Then, the next number decided upon, he puts the cards
back in a pocket, picks up his trombone, and bangs off the
time on the piano. He plays with his eyes open, but sometimes after he has offered an epigrammatic reading of the
melody and is about to improvise he will close his eyes and
disappear. He has the air of an Edwardian bachelor, but he
was married in 1932 to Otealia Foye, whom he first met in
Cincinnati in 1928. They live in Parkchester, in the East
Bronx, and they have never had children.

Dickenson talked about his life this way:

"I was born in Xenia, Ohio, on August 6, 1906. It's about
fifteen miles from Dayton, and it had a population of about
nine thousand. My father, Robert Clarke Dickenson, had
his own plastering business. He was tall, and if anybody
thinks I'm handsome—well, I look like him. He used to play
little ditties on the violin. He died in 1929. My mother was
thin and beautiful, like an angel. They tell me she played
the organ, but I don't remember it. I used to think when I
was little that I wanted to die if my mother died, even
though my father used to let her do the strictness. I believe
she came from Ironton, Ohio, and I believe my father came
from Virginia or West Virginia. There were nine of us
children, and I was the seventh. Arthur, Ernest, Anna, Ed-

ward, Carlos, Walter, Nettie, Edith, and me, Victor. I'm
the only one left. Carlos was a good saxophone player who
ended in the mail service. He was also a thirty-third-degree
Mason. I was proud of that. Another brother fought in the
First World War and worked for International Harvester,
although he was always ailing after the war. One sister died
when she was just about to graduate from college, and another was a schoolteacher. Edith, Ernest, and Walter didn't
survive childhood. We lived in a house on the outskirts of
town, and we had about twelve acres. We tried to raise
corn and such, but the ground was poor. Across the street
from our house was a wood, and the Ku Klux Klan used to
meet there. They'd stand in a circle in their robes in that
wood and burn their crosses, and that upset me all during
my childhood. I was sickly, too. I had pleurisy, and at one
time they thought I was on the verge of t.b., and they had
me go to the t.b. hospital, which put me behind in my
schooling. When I went back to school, they didn't back-
teach me, so I didn't get a chance to learn the things I could
have.

"When I was sixteen or seventeen, I had an accident that
changed my life. I was trying to learn my father's business.
I was carrying a hod full of mortar up a ladder, pulling myself up the rungs with one hand and balancing the hod,
which weighed maybe seventy pounds, with the other. A
rung broke and, with all that weight, I pitched backward,
and gave my back a terrible wrench. I couldn't pick anything up. In fact, I still can't pick much up beyond my
trombone. That accident caused me to decide to become a
musician full time. I had already started playing trombone
in the school band. I tried to play it like a saxophone or
trumpet. I pretended I could read, but what I did was read
the notes the way you read them when you're singing—just
getting the drift of the melody. I played my first job when
I was fifteen, with the Elite Serenaders at an Elks' dance in
Lebanon, Ohio. After that, a bunch of us tried to put a
band together. The center of it was my brother Carlos and
a cousin, Herb Waide, who played piano—but only in the

key of F-sharp. We also had a trumpet player and an alto
saxophonist and a drummer. We had moved to Columbus,
and Carlos and I roomed together. We were on starvation
row. We'd get a gig playing the Saturday matinée in the
movie house and a dance at the Elks' that night, and that
might be it for the week, at three or four dollars a throw.
That wasn't enough to fill a tooth with. We also played occasional gigs with Watkins' Syncopators. Watkins was a
cousin of the bandleader Lloyd Scott and his brother Cecil
Scott. In between jobs with Watkins, I'd work with Tom
Howard, who had the distinction of having his whole band
beaten up by whites in Florida after a dance. I played with
Earl Hood, and travelled around the state, and in 1926 Don
Phillips hired me and I joined him at the Broadway Gardens, in Madison, Wisconsin. His bass player sold me a
trombone, which I needed, for sixty dollars. I was getting
thirty-five a week, and I had to give him fifteen, so that left
me twenty for room and board and everything. At the end
of a month, when I'd finished paying off the bassist, I was
fired, and I didn't have enough money to get back to Columbus. A local drummer I'd met asked me if I knew a piano player he could use that night, and I said I could play
piano in the key of C, so I made enough to get home. I'd
been fired because I couldn't read music, so I vowed after
that to learn to read and write music, and I did. Self-taught—
which I am on the trombone, too. I worked with Bill Broad-
hus in Lexington, Kentucky. Then Helvey's Troubadors
motored down from Cincinnati. J. C. Higginbotham was
in the band, and when he left to go to Buffalo I took his
place. Around this time in Columbus, Lloyd Scott came
through, and he had Dicky Wells, who made a big impression. I also heard Coleman Hawkins and Buster Bailey and
Joe Smith and Louis Armstrong. Jimmy Harrison played a
lot like Louis, and I liked Benny Morton, who played like
Harrison. Of course, when we were kids we listened to
Bessie Smith and Mamie Smith and Ma Rainey and Jelly
Roll Morton—all on records. When the spring broke in the
Victrola, we'd push the turntable around with our fingers
and the music sounded like a sick cow.

"In 1929, I went with Speed Webb, and that was a dag-
gone good band. Roy Eldridge and Teddy Wilson were in
it, and Reunald Jones, who was later with Duke Ellington.
We got as far east as Boston. My aunt was living in Brooklyn, and my mother happened to be staying with her, so I
ducked down to New York. New York fascinated me. I
joined Zack Whyte after Webb, and then went with Thamon
Hayes and his Kansas City Rockets. Harlan Leonard took
over that band after I left. When we were in Memphis in
1933, I got a telegram from Blanche Calloway, and I was
with her three years, before going with Claude Hopkins. I
was with Hopkins until 1939. Jabbo Smith was in Hopkins'
band for a while, and he was something special. He still
played sensationally. I was with Benny Carter's big band
after that. Benny let just about everybody solo, but that
didn't happen in a lot of big bands. You'd sit there week in
and week out, playing those notes, and never get a solo, or
maybe get just eight bars on a bridge, and silence for another couple of weeks. I was with Count Basie for a year
after Carter, and sometimes Basie only gave me one solo a
week, and that was disappointing. Everybody liked each
other in the Basie band. It was like brothers. We were on
the road *all* the time, and in those days you stayed in people's houses, because the hotels wouldn't let you in, so Lester Young and I always tried to find a place together. He
spoke his own language. If he agreed with you, it was 'You
rang the bell—ding ding.' I still say 'Ding ding' before I take
a drink."

Dickenson's style is wasteless and lyrical and funny. He listened to Louis Armstrong in the twenties, as every jazz musician did, and he was much taken by Dicky Wells, whose
work he distantly echoes. High jinks are always around the
corner in his playing. He growls a lot, particularly in ensembles, and the growls add a lazy, bibulous texture to the
counterpoint. He likes to poke fun at fulsome ballads, and
in 1946 he made a classic recording of "You Made Me Love
You," with faultless smears and growls and whispered asides.

Even when he plays the melody of a good song straight, he seems to be laughing up his sleeve. He decorates it with bunched triplets and questioning vibratoless bursts, and he lets the melody run on in the silences in between, like a movie with the soundtrack off. Dickenson doesn't sound like a trombonist. His tone is gentle and downy, and his playing is a direct extension of the way he talks and sings. It has none of the nasal, brassbound sound that affects most trombonists. But when his musical environment gets heated, he plays with great passion. Then he uses staccato phrases, adroit repetitions, emery growls, Dicky Wells shouts, and tumbling curving runs, and he will end his solo with a re-sounding hammerlike note. He invariably swings, and it makes no difference whether he is neighing at a poor ballad or going at top speed. Like all great lyrical workers, he sometimes slides into a slough in which he depends on pat-terns—his triplets and growls and smears—that he has long since perfected. But even these predigested solos are grace-ful and funny. Dickenson's playing has diminished little. He may rely on his patterns more than he once did—they started out, after all, as his inventions—but he also manages to sur-prise you in almost every solo with an oblique cry, a slyly placed silence, a short humming blue note. He likes mutes and he often puts his left hand inside the bell of his horn, making it sound as if he were playing on the other side of the hill. He also hangs a beret over his bell, which gives him a soft, ruffling sound—a bird landing. His dynamics are su-perb. Every solo is a mixture of muted sounds, growls, warning roars, and soft, sliding connective phrases. Many jazz soloists are disconcertingly egocentric. They exude self-pity (Miles Davis), or querulousness (Stan Getz), or dis-dain (Benny Goodman), but Dickenson appears bent on lifting his listeners with humor and warmth and beauty, all the while making it clear that he won't hold us up any longer than is absolutely necessary.

"I play in an unorthodox way," Dickenson said. "I don't lip correctly. You're supposed to put the mouthpiece over your face skin, but I put it on my lip skin, over the inside part of my lip. That's the way I learned, and because of it my chops sometimes wear out, and I can't play the high notes Dicky Wells and Trummy Young do. I do a growl two different ways: I make a strong humming sound in my throat or I do it with special tonguing. There are two sets of positions on the slide that you can get the same notes with—the outer position and the inner position. I get a better sound with the inner position, and I don't have all that weight you have when you use the outer position and the slide pulls the mouthpiece loose. I think about improvising as if I'm singing. It's what I'd do if I were humming. When you improvise, you see your feelings in your mind, and you form certain feelings for numbers that you play over and over. You keep the melody in your mind, too. If you lose it, you can get into an outer-space situation. Sometimes you think a bar ahead, sometimes four bars. If I hit a wrong chord or a wrong note, I try and have a follow-up bar in reserve in my mind to take care of it. Most of that thinking ahead is in rhythmic patterns. A lot of times, you have a framework set up in your head of what you're going to start a solo with and the guy soloing before you doesn't stop when he's supposed to, he dribbles over into your first measure, and that fouls you up and you tell him mentally, Oh, well, hell, go ahead and play another chorus, only stop when you're supposed to. I think maybe I know ten thousand songs. I keep about two or three hundred typed on index cards, which I carry to almost every job as reminders of what to play. They're my repertory cards. If I typed up all the tunes I know, I couldn't carry them with me; they'd be too heavy. I write my own tunes, too, and not one of them has been a hit or has brought in any residuals. Here are some titles: 'Constantly,' 'I'll Try,' 'Mistletoe,' 'What Have You Done with the Key to Your Heart?' Some I have written down but haven't exposed yet.

"Of all the wonderful musicians I've worked with, my happiest days of playing were with Bobby Hackett. We first worked together at the old Child's Paramount in the fifties. We worked together in the fifties and sixties and seventies. Bobby could never manage business things right. He put too much dependence on people, and they took him for what they could. He always trusted the wrong people. He loved to give you things. He'd give you an expensive gift, just like that. I miss him all the time—him and his beautiful, perfect playing.

"If I had it to do over, I'd have a good manager. I'm like Bobby in that respect: I'm a poor businessman. But I know I wouldn't have been a good doctor, and I wouldn't have been a good cook. I know I wouldn't have been a good janitor, and I don't have the patience to be a good teacher. I'd slap them on the finger all the time, and the last thing I ever want to do is mess up my cool. Sometimes I feel like retiring. My ankles swell up after an evening of playing, and my teeth aren't as strong as they used to be. My health is crumbling a little, and I don't like to travel much anymore. I wish I could play when I feel like it and not play when I don't feel like it. In other words, be semi-retired. I would like to have played with Duke Ellington at one time, but he already had such a good trombone player—Lawrence Brown—that I wouldn't have been an addition. I first heard Lawrence Brown play over the air, and he dedicated a number to his mother. I liked that."

Pres

Very little about the tenor saxophonist Lester Young was unoriginal. He had protruding, heavy-lidded eyes, a square, slightly Oriental face, a tiny mustache, and a snaggletoothed smile. His walk was light and pigeon-toed, and his voice was soft. He was something of a dandy. He wore suits, knit ties, and collar pins. He wore ankle-length coats, and pork-pie hats—on the back of his head when he was young, and pulled down low and evenly when he was older. He kept to himself, often speaking only when spoken to. When he played, he held his saxophone in front of him at a forty-five-degree angle, like a canoeist about to plunge his paddle into the water. He had an airy, lissome tone and an elusive, lyrical way of phrasing that had never been heard before. Other saxophonists followed the emperor, Coleman Hawkins, but Young's models were two white musicians: the C-melody saxophonist Frank Trumbauer and the alto saxophonist Jimmy Dorsey—neither of them a first-rate jazz player. When Young died, in 1959, he had become the model for countless saxophonists, white and black, most of whom could play his style better than he could himself. He was a gentle, kind man who never disparaged anyone. He spoke a coded language, about which the pianist Jimmy Rowles has said, "You had to break that code to understand him. It was like memorizing a dictionary, and I think it took me about three months." Much of Young's language has vanished, but here is a sampling: "Bing and Bob" were the police. A "hat" was a woman, and a "homburg" and a "Mexican hat" were types of women. An attractive young girl was a "poundcake." A "gray boy" was a white man, and Young himself, who was light-skinned, was an "oxford gray." "I've got bulging eyes" for this or that meant he approved of something, and "Catalina eyes" and "Watts eyes" expressed high admiration. "Left people" were the fingers of a pianist's left hand. "I feel a draft" meant he sensed a bigot nearby. "Have another helping," said to a colleague on the bandstand, meant "Take another chorus," and "one long" or "two long" meant one chorus or two choruses. People "whispering on" or "buzzing on" him were talking behind his back. Getting his "little claps" meant being applauded. A "zoomer" was a sponger, and a "needle dancer" was a heroin addict. "To be bruised" was to fail. A "tribe" was a band, and a "molly trolley" was a rehearsal. "Can Madam burn?" meant "Can your wife cook?" "Those people will be here in December" meant that his second child was due in December. (He drifted in and out of three marriages, and had two children.) "Startled doe, two o'clock" meant that a pretty girl with doelike eyes was in the right side of the audience.

Eccentrics flourish in crowded, ordered places, and Young spent his life on buses and trains, in hotel rooms and dressing rooms, in automobiles and on bandstands. He was born in Woodville, Mississippi, in 1909, and his family moved almost immediately to Algiers, just across the river from New Orleans. When he was ten, his father and mother separated, and his father took him and his brother Lee and his sister Irma to Memphis and then to Minneapolis. Young's father, who could play any instrument, had organized a family band, which worked in tent shows in the Midwest and Southwest. Young joined the band as a drummer, and then switched to alto saxophone. An early photograph shows him holding his saxophone in much the same vaudeville way he later held it. Young once said that he was slow to learn to read music: "Then one day my father goes to each one in the band and asked them to play their part and I knew that was my ass, because he knew goddam well that I couldn't read. Well, my little heart was broken, you know; I went in crying and I was thinking, I'll come back and catch them, if that's the way they want it. So I went away all by myself and learned the music." Young quit the family band when he was eighteen and joined Art Bronson's Bostonians. During the next six or seven years, he worked briefly in the family band again, and at the Nest Club, in Minneapolis, for Frank Hines and Eddie Barefield. He also worked with the Original Blue Devils and with Bennie Moten, Clarence Love, King Oliver, and, in 1934, Count Basie's first band. In an interview with Nat Hentoff, Young recalled playing with Oliver, who was well into his fifties and at the end of his career:

> After the Bostonians, I played with King Oliver. He had a very nice band and I worked regularly with him for one or two years, around Kansas and Missouri mostly. He had three brass, three reeds, and four rhythm. He was playing well. He was old then and didn't play all night, but his tone was full when he played. He was the star of the show and played one or two songs each set. The blues? He could play some nice blues. He was a very nice fellow, a gay old fellow. He was crazy about all the boys, and it wasn't a drag playing for him at all.

Soon after going with Basie, Young was asked to replace Coleman Hawkins in Fletcher Henderson's band, and, reluctantly, he went. It was the first of several experiences in his life that he never got over. Hawkins had spent ten years with Henderson, and his oceanic tone and heavy chordal improvisations were the heart of the band. Jazz musicians are usually alert, generous listeners, but Young's alto-like tone (he had shifted to tenor saxophone not long before) and floating, horizontal solos sounded heretical to Henderson's men. They began buzzing on him, and Henderson's wife forced him to listen to Hawkins' recordings, in the hope he'd learn to play that way. Young lasted three or four months and went to Kansas City, first asking Henderson for a letter saying that he had not been fired. Two years later, he rejoined Basie, and his career began. The pianist John Lewis knew Young then: "When I was still very young in Albuquerque, I remember hearing about the Young family settling there. They had a band and had come in with a tent show and been stranded. There was a very good local jazz band, called St. Cecilia's, that Lester played in. He also competed with an excellent Spanish tenor player and housepainter named Cherry. I barely remember Lester's playing. He had a fine, thin tone. Then the family moved to Minneapolis, and I didn't see him until around 1934, when he came through on his way to the West Coast to get an alto player for Count Basie named Caughey Roberts. Lester sounded then the way he does on his first recordings, made in 1936. We had a lot of brass beds in that part of the country, and Lester used to hang his tenor saxophone on the foot of his bed so that he could reach it during the night if an idea came to him that he wanted to sound out."

Young's first recordings were made with a small group from Basie's band. The melodic flow suggests Trumbauer and perhaps Dorsey, and an ascending gliss, an upward swoop, that Young used for the next fifteen years suggests Bix Biederbecke. Young had a deep feeling for the blues, and King Oliver's blues must have settled into his bones. He had a pale tone, a minimal vibrato, a sense of silence, long-breathed phrasing, and an elastic rhythmic ease. Until his arrival, most soloists tended to pedal up and down on the beat, their phrases short and perpendicular, their rhythms broken and choppy. Young smoothed out this bouncing attack. He used long phrases and legato rhythms (in the manner of the trumpeter Red Allen, who was in Henderson's band with him), and he often chose notes outside the chords—"odd" notes that italicized his solos. He used silence for emphasis. Young "had a very spacey sound at the end of '33," the bassist Gene Ramey recalls. "He would play a phrase and maybe lay out three beats before he'd come in with another phrase." Coleman Hawkins' solos buttonhole you; Young's seem to turn away. His improvisations move with such logic and smoothness they lull the ear. He was an adept embellisher and a complete improviser. He could make songs like "Willow Weep for Me" and "The Man I Love" unrecognizable. He kept the original melodies in his head, but what came out was his dreams about them. His solos were fantasies—lyrical, soft, liquid—on the tunes he was playing, and probably on his own life as well. The humming quality of his solos was deceptive, for they were made up of quick, virtuosic runs, sudden held notes that slowed the beat almost to a stop, daring shifts in rhythmic emphasis, continuous motion, and often lovely melodies. His slow work was gentle and lullaby-like, and as his tempos rose his tone became rougher and more homemade. Young was also a masterly clarinettist. In the late thirties, he used a metal clarinet (eventually it was stolen, and he simply gave up the instrument), and he got a nudging, murmuring sound. He and Pee Wee Russell resembled each other somewhat, and were the most original clarinettists in jazz.

Young bloomed with Basie. He recorded countless classic solos with the band, giving it a rare lightness and subtlety, and he made his beautiful records accompanying Billie Holiday—their sounds a single voice split in two. Late in 1940, Young decided to go out on his own, as Coleman Hawkins had done years before. He had a small group on Fifty-second Street for a brief time, and went West and put a band together with his brother Lee. The singer Sylvia Syms hung around Young on Fifty-second Street as a teen-ager: "Lester was very light, and he had wonderful hair. He never used that pomade so popular in the forties and fifties. He was a beautiful dresser, and his accent was his porkpie hat worn on the back of his head. He used cologne, and he always smelled divine. Once, I complained to him about audiences who talked and never listened, and he said, 'Lady Syms, if there is one guy in the whole house who is listening—and maybe he's in the *bathroom*—you've got an audience.' His conversation, with all its made-up phrases, was hard to follow, but his playing never was. He phrased words in his playing. He has had a great influence on my singing, and through the years a lot of singers have picked up on him."

Jimmy Rowles worked with Young when he went West: "I don't know when Billie Holiday nicknamed him Pres—for 'the President'—but when I first knew him the band called him Uncle Bubba. Of all the people I've met in this business, Lester was unique. He was alone. He was quiet. He was unfailingly polite. He almost never got mad. If he was upset, he'd take a small whisk broom he kept in his top jacket pocket and sweep off his left shoulder. The only way to get to know him was to work with him. Otherwise, he'd just sit there playing cards or sipping, and if he did say something it stopped the traffic. I never saw him out of a suit, and he particularly liked double-breasted pinstripes. He also wore tab collars, small trouser cuffs, pointed shoes, and Cuban heels. In 1941, the older guard among musicians still didn't recognize his worth. They didn't think of him as an equal. He was *there*, but he was still someone new. And here's an odd thing. His father held a saxophone upside down when he played it, in a kind of vaudeville way, so maybe Lester picked up his way of holding his horn from that. Whichever, the more he warmed up during work, the higher his horn got, until it was actually horizontal."

The Young brothers played Café Society Downtown in 1942, and, after stints with Dizzy Gillespie and the tenor saxophonist Al Sears, Young rejoined Count Basie. He was drafted in 1944, and it was the second experience in his life that he never got over. There are conflicting versions of

what happened, but what matters is that he collided head
on with reality for the first time, and it felled him. He
spent about fifteen months in the Army, mainly in a deten-
tion barracks, for possession of marijuana and barbiturates
and for being an ingenuous black man in the wrong place
at the wrong time. He was discharged dishonorably, and
from then on his playing and his personal life slowly rough-
ened and worsened. John Lewis worked for Young in 1951:
"Jo Jones was generally on drums and Joe Shulman on bass,
and either Tony Fruscella or Jesse Drakes on trumpet. We
worked at places like Bop City, in New York, and we
travelled to Chicago. He would play the same songs in each
set on a given night, but he would often repeat the sequence
the following week this way: if he had played 'Sometimes
I'm Happy' on Tuesday of the preceding week, he would
open 'Sometimes I'm Happy' this Tuesday with a variation
on the solo he had played on the tune the week before; then
he would play variations on the variations the week after,
so that his playing formed a kind of gigantic organic whole.
While I was with him, I never heard any of the coarseness
that people have said began creeping into his playing. I did
notice a change in him in his last few years. There was
nothing obvious or offensive about it. Just an air of depression about him.

"He was a living, walking poet. He was so quiet that
when he talked each sentence came out like a little explo-
sion. I don't think he consciously invented his special language. It was part of a way of talking I heard in Albuquerque from my older cousins, and there were variations
of it in Oklahoma City and Kansas City and Chicago in the
late twenties and early thirties. These people also dressed
well, as Lester did—the porkpie hats and all. So his speech
and dress were natural things he picked up. They weren't a
disguise—a way of hiding. They were a way to be hip—to
express an awareness of everything swinging that was going
on. Of course, he never wasted this hipness on duddish people, nor did he waste good playing on bad musicians. If
Lester was wronged, the wound never healed. Once, at

Bop City, he mentioned how people had always bugged him about the supposed thinness of his tone. We were in his dressing room, and he picked up his tenor and played a solo using this great big butter sound. Not a Coleman Hawkins sound but a thick, smooth, concentrated sound. It was as beautiful as anything I've ever heard."

Young spent much of the rest of his life with Norman Granz's Jazz at the Philharmonic troupe. He had become an alcoholic, and his playing was ghostly and uncertain. He still wore suits and a porkpie hat, but he sat down a lot, and when he appeared on the CBS television show "The Sound of Jazz," in 1957, he was remote and spaced out. He refused to read his parts for the two big-band numbers. (Ben Webster, who had been taught by Young's father, replaced him.) When he took a chorus during Billie Holiday's blues "Fine and Mellow," his tone was intact but the solo limped by. The loving, smiling expression on Billie Holiday's face may have indicated that she was listening not to the Lester beside her but to the Lester long stored away in her head. The tenor saxophonist Buddy Tate drove down with Young from the Newport Jazz Festival the next year: "I first met Lester when he was in Sherman, Texas, playing alto. A little later, I replaced him in the first Basie band when he went to join Fletcher Henderson. He didn't drink then, and he didn't inhale his cigarettes. He was so refined, so sensitive. I was with him in the second Basie band in 1939 and 1940, and he had a little bell he kept on the stand beside him. When someone goofed, he rang it. After the 1958 Newport Festival, I drove back with him to New York, and he was really down. He was unhappy about money, and said he wasn't great. When I told him how great he was, he said, 'If I'm so great, Lady Tate, how come all the other tenor players, the ones who sound like me, are making all the money?' "

The arranger Gil Evans knew Young on the Coast in the forties and in New York at the end of his life: "Solitary people like Lester Young are apt to wear blinders. He concentrated on things from his past that he should have long since set aside as a good or bad essence. The last year of his life, when he had moved into the Alvin Hotel, he brought up the fact that his father had been displeased with him when he was a teen-ager because he had been lazy about learning to read music. But maybe his bringing that up at so late a date was only a vehicle for some other, present anger that he was inarticulate about. Sometimes that inarticulateness made him cry. A long time before, when I happened to be in California, Jimmy Rowles and I went to see Pres, who was living in a three-story house that his father owned. We walked in on a family fight, and Pres was weeping. He asked us to get him out of there, to help move him to his mother's bungalow in West Los Angeles. We had a coupe I'd borrowed, so we did—lock, stock, and barrel. Those tears were never far away. I was with him in the fifties in a restaurant near Fifty-second Street when a man in a fez and robe came in. This man started talking about Jesus Christ, and he called him a prophet. Well, Pres thought he had said something about Jesus and 'profit.' He got up and went out, and when I got to him he was crying. I had to explain what the man had said. I don't know where he got such strong feelings about Jesus. Maybe from going to church when he was young, or maybe it was just his sense of injustice. He couldn't stand injustice of any kind. He had a great big room at the Alvin, and when I'd go up to see him I'd find full plates of food everywhere. They'd been brought by friends, but he wouldn't eat. He just drank wine. One of the reasons his drinking got so out of hand was his teeth. They were in terrible shape, and he was in constant pain. But he was still fussy about things like his hair. He had grown it long at the back, and finally he let my wife, who was a good barber, cut it. At every snip, he'd say, 'Let me see it. Let me see it,' before the hair landed on the floor. It was amazing—a man more or less consciously killing himself, and he was still particular about his hair."

The tenor saxophonist Zoot Sims, who listened hard to Young in the forties, also saw some of this harmless narcissism: "We roomed together on a Birdland tour in 1957, and one day when he was changing and had stripped to his shorts, which were red, he lifted his arms and slowly turned around and said, 'Not bad for an old guy.' And he was right. He had a good body—and a good mind. Lester was a very intelligent man."

Young died at the Alvin Hotel the day after he returned from a gig in Paris. He had given François Postif a long and surprisingly bitter interview while he was in France, and, perhaps wittingly, he included his epitaph in it: "They want everybody who's a Negro to be an Uncle Tom, or Uncle Remus, or Uncle Sam, and I can't make it. It's the same all over: you fight for your life—until death do you part, and then you got it made."

Einfühlung

The defenses of the brilliant, elusive jazz pianist Ellis Larkins seem not so much conscious as a hapless reaction to a precocious childhood. Larkins was born in Baltimore in 1923, and at the age of eleven made his début as a classical pianist by playing a movement of Mozart's Coronation Concerto with the Baltimore City Colored Orchestra, which thrived during the Depression. The newspapers hailed him as a "prodigy" and a "genius," who would rank with "Shura Cherkassky, the other lad whose career was launched in Baltimore." (Prodigies were a big business in the thirties and early forties, and included precocious film stars, the Quiz Kids, twelve-year-old college freshmen, and child vaudevillians like Buddy Rich, Bobby Short, and Sugar Chile Robinson.) A newspaper photograph made of Larkins before the concert resembles a tintype. He is dressed in a dark suit with knickers and a Buster Brown collar with a flowing cravat, and he is standing stolidly beside a grand piano, his left arm draped over the treble end of the keyboard. His hands are much as they are today—big, square, and strong—and so is his masklike face, with its downturned mouth, alarmed, myopic eyes, and windmill ears. During the next five or six years, Larkins, in the manner of the tri-motor literati of the period, was often billed as Ellis Lane Larkins, and he gave a series of appearances, one of which was covered in a Baltimore paper in April of 1937:

> Ellis Larkins, a thirteen-year-old Negro, gave a piano recital in the Common Room at 4:30 o'clock on Sunday, the eighteenth. The recital was sponsored by Mr. Privette. Though it was scheduled for four o'clock, it was half an hour late in starting, because the young pianist arrived a few minutes late.
>
> The program started with a Pastorale by Scarlatti in C Major and contained also Mozart's Sonata in C Major; Seven Preludes, A Flat Major Etude, and Fantaisie Impromptu by Chopin; Brahms' Rhapsody; a Moment Musicale by Schubert; Lento by Cyril Scott; and a Prelude in G Minor by Rachmaninoff.
>
> When questioned after the performance, the young aspirant said, "I don't like to practice." His playing, however, plainly showed that he had practiced very much since he started taking lessons at the age of six. During the whole hour, Larkins had no music before him, but sometimes played so fast that his fingers could not be seen.
>
> When Larkins commenced playing, he had a small audience, but more arrived as the recital continued. His playing was continuous, with only two intermissions of two or three minutes each. To the audience it seemed that he played unlike a young boy, but like a great pianist.

The great pianist would change in certain ways and remain unchanged in others. He still cares little for practicing or for rehearsals (an hour and fifteen minutes is about all he can manage), and he still doesn't use music. But he is punctual nowadays; his hands, though fast, are generally visible; and his two- or three-minute intermissions sometimes last upward of an hour, and divide sets just fifteen or twenty minutes long. Larkins came to New York in 1940 to attend

Juilliard, and before long he began an ongoing retreat into various encircling shadows. To help support himself, he went to work in night clubs, which are eternally dark. (He had learned jazz from recordings and from frequent visits to the Royal Theatre, in Baltimore, where the big bands played.) He tried being a sideman, and even a leader, and then slipped into the near-anonymity of accompanying singers. In the mid-fifties, he vanished into the studios as an accompanist and vocal coach, and except for a short turn with Larry Adler in 1959 he didn't reappear until 1972, when he took a job as a solo pianist at Gregory's. But his mini sets and maxi intermissions made it seem as if he were barely there. He lasted at Gregory's surprising two years, and after that he flitted from The Cookery to Michael's Pub to Tangerine to Hopper's to Larson's to Daly's Daffodil before settling down at the Carnegie Tavern, at Fifty-sixth and Seventh Avenue.

Larkins' style gives the impression of continually being on the verge of withdrawing, of bowing and backing out. It is uncommonly gentle. His touch is softer than Art Tatum's, and the flow of his melodic line has a rippling, quiet-water quality. Nothing is assertive: his chords, in contrast to the extroverted cloud masses that most pianists use, turn in and muse; his single-note lines shoot quickly to the left or the right and are gone; his statements of the melody at the opening and closing of each number offer silhouettes. But Larkins' serenity is deceptive, for his solos have a strong rhythmic pull. It is clear that he once listened attentively to Earl Hines and Teddy Wilson, and possibly to Jess Stacy. Larkins' short, precise, dashing arpeggios suggest Wilson, and so do the even, surging tenths he uses in his left hand. He attempts a vibrato effect by adding the barest tremolo to the end of certain right-hand phrases, recalling Stacy and the early Hines. His intent is immediate pleasure—for the listener and for himself—and it is also to celebrate the songs he plays. He endows and sustains them, indirectly fulfilling a nice maxim laid down not long ago by the drummer Art Blakey. "Music," Blakey said, "should wash away the dust of everyday life." There is probably no better accompanist than Larkins. When a singer accepts accompaniment, he asks the accompanist to take over part of the arduousness of performing, for which he repays the accompanist by excelling. The perfect singer-accompanist relationship is contrapuntal. The singer creates one melodic line and the accompanist another line: they move separately but indivisibly. Larkins provides an aura for the singer—a constant cushion of chords, melodic suggestions, dynamics, and rhythmic pushes and retards. He anticipates and celebrates the singer, guessing unerringly where the singer will take the melody next and applauding apt phrases. He embraces the singer without touching him and leads him without pointing. Accompanying provides Larkins with what he has sought since childhood: to be an indispensable second voice.

The singer Anita Ellis rarely uses any other accompanist. One afternoon, she and Larkins rehearsed for an album they were soon to record. Larkins arrived at Anita Ellis's apartment, on the upper East Side, at one o'clock sharp. He was dressed in a gray Glen plaid suit and a bright-yellow sports shirt—an ensemble that resembled a muffled yell. Larkins talks as little as possible, but when he does talk he issues clumps of words. Some are intelligible and others he swallows, leaving curves of sound that have more to do with music than with words. But he offers help in the form of hand signals, which he hoists once or twice during almost every utterance. These are the shadows of his words, spoken and unspoken, and they are a pleasure to watch, for they flicker and insinuate and dance. Larkins still has a boyish figure. His stomach protrudes, and his back is concave. His arms and legs are spindly, and he has long, anchoring feet. He wears heavy, protective horn-rimmed glasses, and his only expressions are a smile that passes over his face so quickly that his teeth never show and a flaring of the eyes that he uses when an exclamation point is needed.

Before he sat down at the piano, which he addresses flawlessly—his back straight, his knees just below the keyboard, his elbows clamped to his sides—he cracked all his knuckles and violently shook each hand at the floor, as if he were a swimmer forestalling cramps. Anita Ellis, got up in a white Castelbajac blouse and white pants, stationed herself behind the piano. She said she had talked that morning with Gil Wiest, the owner of the Carnegie Tavern and of Michael's Pub, where she and Larkins held forth for seven classic weeks in the fall of 1974. "He told me that you're a complete gentleman, Ellis," she said in her lyrical, quickstep way of talking. "And that you pack them in."

Larkins opened his mouth in mock amazement and held up three fingers. "I haven't seen Gil for three months," he said. "He leaves me absolutely alone."

"All right, Ellis," she laughed. "Shall we do Burke and Van Heusen—'But Beautiful'?" She sang, "Love is funny or it's sad, or it's quiet or it's mad," and Larkins began pedalling beside her, supplying coloring chords and anticipatory runs. He took an eight-bar solo, and, as is his wont, mouthed the lyrics as he improvised. She went into a sudden crescendo in the last eight bars, and they finished quietly.

She put the music of Duke Ellington's "Prelude to a Kiss" on the piano, and Larkins played the first eight bars in slow, legato fashion. He stopped, and she said, "You do that so laid back it's marvellous. I want to try it, too. Will that interfere?"

He shook his head and began, and she sang with him. He stopped at the end of four bars. "That's *too* far behind, Anita," he said. He began again, and she followed more closely. His chords moved along with her, and he led her into the bridge with a bright cluster of single notes, and at the close of the bridge he paused and said, "Should I wait for you?"

"You don't have to wait for me, Ellis."

He finished the chorus and said, "You were too far behind."

"I haven't been listening to you. I've just been doing my thing."

They did one more chorus, and at its end she inserted four bars of humming. They were slightly off pitch, as she had been in several places in the song. "The trouble with that song," Larkins said, "is that if one tone goes off, it all seems to go off." She nodded and laughed.

They did a slow, delicate, almost transparent version of Billy Strayhorn's "A Flower Is a Lovesome Thing." The melody, as in most of Strayhorn's pieces, has a misterioso quality, and it moves in long, gradual steps. It is not a singer's song, and when they had finished she said, "We'll go back to that next week. I don't know, I can't seem to *find* that song. I can't seem to get it in place. Maybe it should be a half tone higher."

Larkins shrugged and, holding one hand horizontally over his head, raised it an inch. "Maybe we can try it in a different key," he said.

They did buoyant, swinging versions of "Spring Will Be a Little Late This Year" and Stephen Sondheim's "Anyone Can Whistle." She sang forcefully, and Larkins grew appropriately loud, and on the last eight bars of "Whistle," when she sang "I can slay a dragon" Larkins churned and boiled, leaning on his loud pedal and moving his shoulders up and down.

"Wheeeee," Anita Ellis cried. "Let's take five."

Larkins went to the kitchen to get a drink, and when he got back she said, "Ellis, after this album let's do one with just bar songs, the songs that any old piano player and singer used to sing in any old bar—songs like 'I Don't Want to Cry Any More' and 'You've Changed' and 'You Don't Know What Love Is.' "

Larkins nodded and opened his eyes very wide.

"Speaking of bars," she said, "I saw 'The Joe Louis Story' the other night on television. Do you remember that, Ellis? We were in a bar scene, and I sang 'I'll Be Around.' I think the producer had heard us do it at the Village Vanguard. We were much better than I thought. They filmed it at Grossinger's, and we met Louis."

Larkins nodded and made a single fist in the air.

They did Alec Wilder's "Who Can I Turn To," and Larkins gave it extra sparkle just before the bridge by slipping in a sleek arrangement of double-time chords which had the effect of throwing Anita Ellis's words into graceful slow motion. "I love to do that song," Anita Ellis said. "It's such a collaboration. Let's do 'Summertime,' Ellis."

"Let's wait until next time," he said, a smile flickering across his face.

She ignored him, and began the song a cappella. Larkins joined her with loose chords and a sprinkle of ascending single notes. They created a sense of "quietude," which she had earlier said she wanted in the album. But when she sang "One of these mornings, you're going to rise up singing" she gave a startling shout that Larkins answered with quick, heavy chords. The thunder died away, and she hummed the repeat ending of the song, and the two pure and beautiful voices—voice and piano—crossed and recrossed one another.

A Basie-like "I Hear Music," with a lot of galloping Larkins chords, was followed by a bluesy "Moanin' in the Mornin' " and a studied, careful "Out of This World," which slid in and out of tempo.

Larkins struck a final chord and jumped to his feet. He offered Anita Ellis his delicate handshake and said, "That's it. It won't do any good, but I have to take my beauty nap. I'll be here next week." He was in the elevator before the front door had closed. An hour and twenty-two minutes had elapsed since his arrival.

Anita Ellis crossed her living room and sat by a picture window that looks over Carl Schurz Park and the East River. "The most remarkable thing about Ellis is that he has such *Einfühlung*—such in-feeling, or sympathy. He really feels *with* you. I can change my way of doing a song and not say anything to him, and he will catch it immediately. I *think* all the time when I sing, making up my own stories behind the songs. The song isn't Alec Wilder or Burton Lane any longer. Ellis understands this, and the song becomes just Ellis and me and what's going on in my head. Theatre singers don't generally like Ellis. He's not a pounder. He's too inventive, too corrective. If he finds what he considers a weak chord in a song, he changes it. He listens and invents. He composes all the time. And he doesn't compromise. He plays and you have to *sing*. Of course, a temperament goes with all his sensitivity. Sometimes his mind is just on other things and he clump-clump-clumps. But that's rare, and I can usually jolly him out of it.

"I first met him at the Blue Angel around 1950. When he played for me, I realized he was *there*, and I became freer than I'd ever been before. He was quiet and gentlemanly, but you knew right away that he was a feelingful and articulate man. He'd call me once in a while, sounding so tentative, and ask me if I'd like to go down to Bon Soir with him and hear Mildred Bailey sing, and he'd tell me how much he liked to accompany her and what a fine musician she was. My opening night at the Blue Angel, I was so frightened that he sent me flowers and said I was the best singer he'd ever heard. He lived in a hotel in the West Forties, and I think he led a very Spartan life. There were always pretty ladies around, but they didn't seem to be *with* him. He was always just Ellis. Although he has been married twice, you don't think of Ellis as having a life outside music. His friends are mostly musicians, and when he isn't playing or with them he's watching television or he's asleep. In the late fifties or early sixties, he had a son. When the child was two or three, Ellis would take him to rehearsals, and I think he was a genius—a miniature Ellis. Once, I had to rehearse a Japanese song, with all these quarter tones, and I was having a time of it, but Ellis's little boy sang the notes just like that. The child became his lifeline. Ellis is rather remote, but to see him on a piano bench with his son right beside him was a rare oneness. It reminded me of a drummer I'd seen in the jungle in British Guiana on a trip with my husband. The man sat there hitting this great drum with his huge hands, and all the while his little son, who was folded into his lap, kept his hands right on top of his father's. But Ellis's son was suddenly taken away from him by the child's mother, and Ellis didn't know what to do. Finally, he went to the Coast to get away from here, and he worked for Joe Williams. After he came back, in the early seventies, the boy reappeared, and Ellis was beside himself. Then, not so long after, the boy was killed in a motorcycle accident in Montreal. It was a dark, destructive, tragic thing. But Ellis goes on, and he plays as beautifully as ever and looks as elegant as ever. Ellis is never dégagé. He has an air about him that makes certain people feel better about liking jazz. I sometimes think of Ellis's playing as being so of a piece that it comes down to one note—one perfect, hypnotic note."

Larkins arrived at work that night a few minutes before eight. He wore a tuxedo with a ruffled shirt. He ordered a brandy at the bar and sat down with some friends on a banquette opposite the bandstand. It has been clear since he opened there that the Carnegie Tavern is just right for him. It has a first-rate piano—a brittle but brilliant August Förster, made in East Germany. The room is warm but impersonal, and is done up in a variety of safe browns, lit by occasional mirrors. It is spacious enough to absorb Larkins' coterie—which, paradoxically, can be fervent and noisy— and retain its composure. Larkins moved to the piano at eight-fifteen. He cracked his knuckles and shook out his hands, and started a medium "Stormy Weather." He often does medleys at the Tavern, and when "I've Got the World on a String" followed, it was plain he was into Harold Arlen. "I Gotta Right to Sing the Blues" came next, and by the close it was also clear that so far he was only idling, that he was, perhaps, somewhere else and would in all probability not be back until the next set. Everything in his style was in place— the cycling tenths, the shapely chords, the reverence for melody—but it was in soft focus. "Ill Wind" gave way to "Come Rain or Come Shine," and he completed the set, which lasted twenty minutes, with a careful "Blues in the Night."

Larkins sat down at a table near the piano with an admirer from New Zealand who was passing through New

York and had spent the four nights of his visit listening to Larkins. The New Zealander asked Larkins why he hadn't made a solo recording in twenty years, and Larkins explained that in 1973 he had recorded enough material for Ernest Anderson, the public-relations man and old-time jazz fan, to fill seven L.P.s, but the editing hadn't even been done. The New Zealand man said he had heard that Larkins had been a child prodigy and asked if he would talk about his childhood.

Larkins let loose a barrage of abstract hand signals, looked quickly over his left shoulder, and stared briefly at the man. Then he shrugged, and said, in approximate translation, "I was the oldest of six children, of whom three boys and one girl are left [*counts off four fingers of his right hand*]. My father was short and stocky and very strict. He did catering and janitoring, and sometimes he'd take me with him. He was also a violinist, and he played with the Baltimore City Colored Orchestra and Chorus, which was formed in 1931 or 1932. He started me on violin when I was two, and he began showing me notes on the piano when I was four. I'd spin one of those piano stools as high as it would go, and perch on top [*rapid spinning motions with his right forefinger*]. The Baltimore City Colored Orchestra played at various high schools for black audiences, although whites were welcome. I'd go with my father to rehearsals and play cymbals and triangle [*holds an imaginary triangle in the air with his left thumb and forefinger, and makes striking motions with his right hand*], and, when I got old enough, violin and assistant piano. My first piano teacher was Joseph Privette, and I went to him through a Dr. Bloodgood, whom my father worked for. Then I studied with Privette's teacher, Austin Conradi, and eventually with Pasquale Tallarico and Gladys Mayo. I made my début with the Baltimore Orchestra when I was just eleven, and I gave a lot of recitals after that in churches and schools and at friends' houses. My father arranged everything. Both my parents were born in Baltimore. My mother was a quiet, pretty, easygoing person, and she played the piano. One day when I came home

from school, she was playing a hymn and I told her it was
in the wrong key, and she said, 'That's right, but I just
transposed it' [*rolls his eyes and cocks his head*]. So she
knew what she was doing. Between 1936 and 1938, when I
was in high school, I also studied at the Peabody Conservatory. But I was aware of what was going on on the other
side of the fence. I heard a lot of jazz on the radio [*cups one
ear, as if listening*]—Fats Waller and Count Basie and Earl
Hines and Teddy Wilson—and I caught all the big bands at
the Royal Theatre. I graduated from high school in 1940
and came directly to New York to attend Juilliard, where I
had a three-year scholarship. This came about through a
young divinity student in Baltimore named Godwin who'd
heard me play and brought me to Juilliard to audition. I
lived on Manhattan Avenue with a woman whose mother
was in our congregation in Baltimore, where I'd been an
altar boy and all that [*pats the top of his head with one
hand*]. When I came to New York, I had every intention of
being a classical pianist, but I started working as a jazz
pianist simply out of the need for money. The guitarist Billy
Moore heard me and told John Hammond, who got me into
the union. I joined Moore's trio, and we went to Cleveland.
I was still at Juilliard, and my teacher told me he didn't care
what I played so long as I didn't lose my *approach* to the
instrument. I didn't hear Art Tatum until I came to New
York. The first time was at an after-hours place uptown.
All the pianists there played, then Tatum sat down with his
beer next to him and washed them all away [*pretends to
clear the tabletop with one vigorous sweep of his hands*].
I went into Café Society Uptown with Billy Moore on
September 14, 1942, and when he got sick in December I
took over with a trio made up of Bill Coleman on trumpet
and Al Hall on bass. Teddy Wilson had a sextet there, too,
with Emmett Berry and Ed Hall and Benny Morton and
Sid Catlett, and we alternated playing for dancing between
the floor shows. If Teddy got sick, I'd replace him. I went
into the Dubonnet in Newark, and Max Gordon came all
the way over to ask me to come into his Blue Angel. I was

there with the trio a year. In 1945, I went back to Café Society with Ed Hall, who had taken over the band, and after that I divided my time between the Blue Angel and the Village Vanguard [*makes piano-playing motions in the air to his right, then to his left*]. The Blue Angel closed in the early sixties, and rock came in, and I went into the studios as an accompanist and a vocal coach. It kept me alive through the fifties and sixties, and in 1968 I moved to the Coast and became Joe Williams' accompanist."

The New Zelander thanked Larkins and asked him how he liked being an accompanist.

Larkins nodded his head quickly up and down once, and looked at his watch. "I first comped for my father when I was five or six, and in high school I played for vocal groups and did a little arranging. I try and keep my ear alert and I try and keep myself aware of the lyric. After a while, you sense where a singer is going and where she isn't. You lead her and you keep out of her way. The two voices—the pianist's and the singer's—should move side by side and contrapuntally, and it becomes a little game between them [*shakes cupped hands, as if they contained dice*]. I can play by myself anytime, but it is a great challenge to play off of someone else. I never lose the melody when I play solo. I give the melody at the beginning of a song and at the end. In between, when I improvise, I make little melodies of my own, and it becomes a way of expressing myself, of improving the original—you hope [*opens his eyes wide*]. Three things go on in my head when I solo: the melody; the lyrics, which I say to myself as I go along; and a kind of imaginary big band, which directs the voicings—the chords I play—so that some will resemble the reed section and some the brass. I also see things impressionistically in my head [*shields his eyes scout-fashion with one hand*], and this is triggered by certain words in the lyrics. The word 'shimmering' in 'Autumn in New York' makes me see shimmering leaves and shimmering lights, and the light lyrics of 'Bidin' My Time' make me see life just rocking easily along. But some songs you leave alone, some songs you can't improve, and you just play them and get out—songs like 'Willow Weep for Me' and 'Someone to Watch Over Me' and 'The Man I Love.' "

Larkins checked his watch again, and excused himself. He went to the piano and into a Gershwin medley, and it was immediately apparent that he was back. He experimented with time all through the set, playing an exquisite slow "I Got Rhythm" and a rocking " 'S Wonderful." He did "The Man I Love" at three different speeds, keeping the melody clear and in the forefront, and he did an ad-lib "Lady Be Good." "Someone to Watch Over Me" was precise and languorous, and he closed with a medium, extended "I've Got a Crush on You," which he made into a love song and a hymn and a lullaby. Then, in one unbroken motion, he stood up, bowed and clapped his hands to the applause, dropped down the bandstand steps, and covered the four feet to the bar, where he held up one tall finger.

Being a Genius

Harold Rosenberg once wrote, "Folk art stands still. It neither aspires upward, like academic painting, nor advances forward, like the inventions of the modernist art movements . . . No one is anyone else's forerunner, and the question of who did it first . . . does not arise. All works of folk art exist simultaneously in the peaceable kingdom of individual imaginings and skill." Rosenberg was writing of the great American primitive painters—and tinsmiths, carpenters, furniture-makers, potters, and wood-carvers—of the eighteenth and nineteenth centuries. But his words also apply to the jazz musicians and jazz singers and tap dancers who, untutored, irrepressible, obsessed, have sprung from every American climate and soil during the past seventy or eighty years. One of the most startling and original members of this primitive army, which includes Duke Ellington and Louis Armstrong and Charlie Parker, was the pianist Erroll Garner.

Garner was born in Pittsburgh, and died in Los Angeles,

in 1977, at the age of fifty-three. His sister, Martha Murray, has said of the Garner family: "Mother was born in Staunton, Virginia, and she graduated from Avery College, here in Pittsburgh. She was a quiet person who got a lot out of life. She had patience. She would never speak down on anybody. She had humor. She had that insight into people, and she had profound wisdom. She took an interest in everything we children did. She saw good in everybody, and she lived by 'Do unto others as you would have them do unto you.' She was about five foot five, and she had a round face and a very pleasant smile. She had beautiful eyes, but later in her life she lost her sight. She never complained or was reproachful. She never lost her serenity. In fact, you wouldn't have believed she was blind. When one of us walked down the street with her she moved straight along. She didn't use a cane, and she didn't feel with her feet. She didn't lose her timing. She had a fine contralto voice, and she and Father sang in the church choir. Father had a lovely tenor voice, and he also sang in a quartet. He had wanted to be a concert singer, but he suffered from asthma. He was about the same height as my mother, but he was slight-built. He was outgoing and had a marvelous sense of humor. He liked to dress well at all times, and at Easter he wore a morning coat and striped trousers. He was the essence of perfection when it came to that.

"We lived in a brick row house on North St. Clair, in the East Liberty section of Pittsburgh. It was owned by our church, and we had two floors in the center house. The church sat a block away, on Euclid Avenue. I was the oldest, then there was my brother Linton, and Ruth, who lives in Pasadena, and Berniece, who still lives in Pittsburgh. Erroll was the baby of the family. He started playing the piano between the ages of two and three—with both hands. Father had given Mother a Victrola, which had beautiful mahogany wood, and Mother would play recordings at our bedtime. The next morning, Erroll would pull himself up on the piano stool and play exactly what he had heard the night before. Miss Madge Bowman taught us all piano—Erroll excepted. When she played a new number to show us how it would sound when we learned it, Erroll would play the number right off after she had gone. He kind of took lessons from her for a while, but he never could learn to read. Miss Madge was a graduate of the Pennsylvania College for Women, and she was an accomplished teacher. Finally, she took Erroll to Carnegie Tech and had him play for the professors, and they told her that there was no need for him to read music, that he would play the same whether he learned or not. He was your average rascally boy, but he was friendly with everybody, and, being a genius, he was invited by everybody to play their pianos. Of course, pianos were very fashionable then, and you didn't have a home if you didn't have a piano. Because Erroll's legs were so short, he completely wore out the panel below the keyboard of our piano by keeping time on it with his feet. We came out of a household where we entertained every Sunday—Linton and I washed many a dish behind company. I do remember that a Mr. Duckett—Mr. William Duckett, I believe—was one of the people who would stop by. He lived in Boston, but his parents lived in our neighborhood, and when he visited them he came to our house and played the piano. Everybody sat so quiet you would have thought we were in a concert hall. He played excellent ragtime, and he'd play three or four numbers. It was simple things like that that the whole family got a kick out of—in particular, Erroll. Mother used to say after Erroll had left home that she thought he never had realized when he was young just how much he *did* play. When he did realize what his gift was, he never got to the point where he was too good to speak to his old Pittsburgh friends."

Linton Garner lives in Vancouver, British Columbia, and is a professional pianist. He has said, "Our father was named Ernest, and he was from North Carolina. He was in maintenance with the Westinghouse Company. He played saxophone and guitar and mandolin, and he'd had a band. My mother, Estella, was strong and solid and stout. We were poor people. It was rough at times, but we never went

through that starvation period. Our parents always had
enough for us to eat. We had a good home. The house was
full of music and full of friends. Erroll had that kind of
lightning mind where he could play anything he heard.
When he heard a player piano somewhere, he'd come home
and imitate all those old trills and tremolos. We listened to
Earl Hines and Art Tatum and Teddy Wilson, and Fats
Waller was strong with us, too."

Erroll Garner went to junior and senior high school at
Westinghouse High. Carl McVicker was director of in-
strumental music, and he once said of Garner, "Besides
Erroll, I had Billy Strayhorn and Fritzy Jones, who later
became Ahmad Jamal. Fritzy didn't like playing for people,
and he'd put his head in his hands when he had to. Strayhorn
liked to play in public, and so did Erroll. In fact, he was
crazy about entertaining. He had a low I.Q., so he was put
in an ungraded class run by Mrs. Lyons—naturally, we
called it the Lyons Den. She taught her students the basics
of math and reading and writing. When Erroll wasn't with
Mrs. Lyons, he played the piano by the hour, or played
tuba in the band, which he picked up by ear. Erroll was a
lovely boy, and he was absolutely no nuisance. He was with
us from 1936 until 1940. One time, when I was rehearsing
the stage band for the show we gave every spring, we hit a
part in the stock arrangement we were using that our pianist
just couldn't get the hang of. The kids started saying, 'Let
Erroll try! Let Erroll try!' Erroll was sitting in the back
listening, and since he couldn't read I didn't see what help
he could be, but I told him to come up and try. He sat
down and improvised a passage that was three times better
that what was written in the score, so we used him."

Garner was short and was shaped like a wedge. He had
fullback shoulders and long arms. His hands were rangy and
long-fingered and loose. They moved like thieves on the keyboard. He wore his hair patent-leather style, and he had
a narrow face and a beaked nose. He looked like a pirate.
He had a blue-black beard and a huge brush mustache and
heavy-lidded eyes. When he played, his music was refracted

through his face and body. His body kept time. He gave
ecstatic smiles, popped his eyes, made "O"s with his mouth,
and peered crazily at his sidemen, his eyes half shut with
delight. All the while, he issued a stream of loud basso-
profundo rhythmic grunts.

There was little waste in Garner's career. He came to
New York in 1944. He worked at the Melody Bar, on
Broadway, and at the Rendezvous, and Jimmy's Chicken
Shack, uptown. Then he landed at Tondelayo's, on Fifty-
second Street, and he was off. Here are three voices from
that time. The first belongs to the bassist Slam Stewart:
"Around 1944, I had John Collins, the guitarist, and Art
Tatum in a trio at the Three Deuces, on Fifty-second Street.
Tatum took sick, and I asked Erroll Garner to fill in for
him. Erroll was working as a single down the street at Tondelayo's, and he'd play a set there and then come over and
play a set with us, and he fell right in wonderfully. They
let him leave Tondelayo's, and he worked with us full time.
We were together a year and a half or two years, and we
had many a good time together. We built a pure friendship,
and we were always talking about our music and what we
were going to play next."

The second is John Collins': "I heard Erroll in Pittsburgh
around 1941. I was with Fletcher Henderson's band, and I
heard him in some little club. He was already different, he
was already a stylist, and that is surely one mark of great-
ness. Everybody else was going the bebop way and all, but
Erroll went his own route and stuck to it. What I think I
admired most about him in Pittsburgh was the way he
mopped his face with his handkerchief. He wiped it between measures, and he never missed a beat. I worked with
him in Slam Stewart's trio on Fifty-second Street and in
Paris. When we got off the plane, there was a big reception
committee, and we thought it was for Coleman Hawkins,
who was with us and was coming back to Paris for the first
time since 1939. But it was for Erroll. He'd already won
some kind of prize, and they were there to honor him. In
the seventies, he moved out to the Coast, where I had lived
a long time, and he was very strange. I only saw him once,

and that was when he sat in at a place where I was playing. He looked fine and he played marvellously. But I never saw him again, or even heard from him, and I think it was because he was already ill and didn't want anybody to know. He never liked to dwell on the dark side of things."

The third voice belongs to Sylvia Syms: "The first time I saw Erroll Garner, he had that patent-leather hair and that smile in his eyes, and he was wearing an old blue overcoat that might have belonged to his father and was too long. Art Tatum had sent him as a courier to bring me a little glass piano with his and my initials on it. When it broke, Tatum replaced it with one from Van Cleef & Arpels, which I finally gave to Erroll, because he pestered me so long about it. Tatum told me that he adored Erroll, and that was strange, because they were so different. Tatum was something of a stuffed shirt, while Erroll was so articulate in his street-smart way. Erroll loved chubby ladies. I ran into him once after I had taken off about forty pounds, and he looked at me with his head on one side and said, 'You shouldn't have ought to have done it, Sylvia.' Later, after I'd gained it back, he said, 'Now, that's how a woman should look.' He was a very generous man. I remember walking to Jilly's with him in the sixties and I don't know how many times he stopped to say, 'Hey, baby,' and reach into his pocket and lay something on whoever it was. But he was already doing that in the forties in the White Rose Bar at Sixth Avenue and Fifty-second Street."

By 1950, his career had been taken over by Martha Glaser, who made Garner famous. During the next twenty-five years, he worked an endless round of concerts (many with symphony orchestras), night clubs, and television appearances. He also made thousands of recordings. Recording studios tend to stymie jazz musicians, but Garner bloomed in them. This is George Avakian's description of a 1953 Columbia recording session:

> Erroll rattled off thirteen numbers, averaging over six minutes each . . . with no rehearsal and no retakes. Even with a half-hour pause for coffee, we were finished twenty-

seven minutes ahead of the three hours of normal studio
time—but Erroll had recorded over eighty minutes of music
instead of the usual ten or twelve, and . . . his performance could not have been improved upon. He asked to
hear playbacks on two of the numbers, but only listened to
a chorus or so of each before he waved his hand.

The drummer Kelly Martin worked with Garner in the
fifties and sixties: "I joined Erroll in Pittsburgh in 1956 and
left him in Pittsburgh in 1966. Shadow Wilson had been
Erroll's drummer before me, and he told me, 'You got to
watch Erroll all the time. You got to listen and watch.'
Erroll liked to have his bass player sit on his left, so that
the bass player could see his left hand. And he liked to have
his drummer sit so he could see the drummer's hands. His
way of playing and creating was all in his face, and his
way of talking was in the piano. He hardly said anything to
the audience, he never even introduced his sidemen. If he
was going to take an intermission, he'd make a little series of
upward notes at the end of a piece, and we'd know. If he
was down or upset, we could hear it in his playing. There
were all kinds of secrets. Once, we were having a drink together between sets, and when my glass was empty I started
playing on it with the swizzlestick—*chink-de-chink, chink-
de-chink*. So Erroll started the first number of the next set
in the key that the swizzlestick made on the glass. Erroll
didn't like to rush into what he was going to play, and those
long, crazy introductions gave him time to settle himself.
We almost never knew what he would play, but we got so
we could almost think in his vein. He loved people, and he
loved to play for them. When we hit a loud crowd, he'd
handle them by playing softer and softer until finally his
hands were actually just *above* the keyboard. Then somebody would notice that Erroll wasn't making any sound at
all and would shush the racket, and Erroll would lower his
hands onto the keys and pick up where he'd left off. We
almost always wore tuxedos. Eddie Calhoun, who played
bass most of the time I was with Erroll, used to say, 'Man,
it's hard to swing in a tuxedo,' and I seconded that. Erroll

could make anybody swing, though. We played a concert in this big, beautiful hall in Helsinki, and before we started that audience was so stiff you could hear it breathing. After the first number, there was a sharp lull—then here come the hands.

"Erroll's mother was blind when I met her, but she was a well-adjusted woman. I met Erroll's father at the same time, and we stole away from the crowd to some Class D bar where the bartender knew him and would give him enough whiskey in the glass so he could at least see it. Erroll told me once that he thought he'd rather be blind than deaf, because he played by sound and he didn't have to see out of his ear to hear. Sometimes he'd make up whole new tunes during a performance, and he'd grin at Calhoun and me and growl in that voice, 'Stick with me, stick with me.' "

Garner also "wrote" songs, some of them striking. He told the drummer Art Taylor in "Notes and Tones" how he had written "Misty":

> I wrote "Misty" from a beautiful rainbow I saw when I was flying from San Francisco to Chicago. At that time, they didn't have jets and we had to stop off in Denver. When we were coming down there was a beautiful rainbow. This rainbow was fascinating because it wasn't long but very wide and in every color you can imagine. With the dew drops and the windows being misty, that fine rain, that's how I named it "Misty." I was playing on my knees like I had a piano, with my eyes shut. There was a little old lady sitting next to me and she thought I was sick because I was humming. She called the hostess, who came over, to find out I was writing "Misty" in my head. By the time I got off the plane, I had it. We were going to make a record date, so I put it right on that date. I always say that wherever she is today that old lady was the first one in on "Misty."

Garner's sound was by turns robust and delicate, rococo and spare, "down" and sentimental, discordant and melodic, driving and lackadaisical. Every number was an adventure. You knew certain stylistic flourishes would appear—the on-the-beat left-hand chords (possibly inspired by his days as a tubist); the right-hand tremolos (echoes, perhaps, of player-piano rolls); the stiff-legged, staccato single-note lines in the right hand; the startling dynamics; the spinning, funny, tantalizing introductions, some of them a dozen or more bars in length and complete iconoclastic compositions in themselves; the octave chords; and the fragments of parody and interpolation—but you never knew when or in what combination. Garner constantly surprised his listeners and himself. You would hear him suddenly drop into several choruses of stride piano (having never heard him play any before), and do it with a rocking, irresistible ease. You'd hear him play a delicate melodic chorus, break off and go into an eighteen- or twenty-bar arrhythmic passage, in which each hand spun out a different, almost atonal single-note line, and pick up the melody again. You'd hear him play thunderous chords and drop into a legato right-hand figure that was so soft a cat would walk right by. You'd hear him turn an up-tempo ballad into a wild rhythm ma-chine—the left hand hammering steadily, the right hand high heels on marble. Garner, like all great primitives, was trapped inside his style, but he never allowed it to harden into self-parody. He kept reaching farther and farther into the mysterious area where his uniqueness had come from. Garner does not sound like any other jazz pianist; whatever there once was of Earl Hines or Teddy Wilson or Fats Waller had long been abstracted. But the colors and vivid-ness and originality of Garner's playing have been so en-compassing that there are few pianists who don't at one time or another sound like him.

The pianist Jimmy Rowles has spoken of Garner: "I don't think there is a jazz pianist, young or old, who hasn't been influenced by Erroll Garner. He laid down his own little laws, and everyone obeyed. I met him around 1950, when he was playing solo piano at the Haig in Los Angeles. He was just starting that left-hand four-four, *thrum-thrum-thrum-thrum* thing, using his left hand as a full rhythm sec-tion. I was working across the street at the Ambassador with the Modernaires or some group like that, and I'd listen to him between sets. He liked to kind of growl when he talked, and I think I learned to growl from him. When Erroll walked into a room, a light went on. He was an imp. He could make poor bass players and poor drummers play like champions. When he played, he'd sit down and drop his hands on the keyboard and start. He didn't care what key he was in or anything. He was a full orchestra, and I used to call him Ork. When he was at the Haig, he'd come over after his set and say, 'What do you think? Do you think I'm right or wrong?' and laugh. And I'd always say, 'You're right, Ork. You're right.' "

The pianist and arranger Sy Johnson has also studied his Garner: "A famous classical pianist once told Erroll that he should record all the time—that he shouldn't wait for recording dates and such but should go into a recording studio whenever he got a chance and capture what his head was always full of. One time, he went into a studio and played for hour after hour. Just by himself—no bass and drums, which he never needed anyway. The tape that came out of it is the most amazing solo jazz piano I have ever heard. *Everything* on it is a tour de force. It is a man taking endless chances. It is tapping a keg and out comes a torrent. He had astonishing hands. He could write—sign autographs— with both hands. His hands used to unfold on the keyboard and keep going, and he is supposed to have been able to reach a thirteenth. What distinguished him from every other jazz piano player, though, was his rich and profound quality of time. He could play a totally different rhythm in each hand and develop equally what he was doing in each hand. He was way down deep in the time thing. He was this magnificent pianistic engine."

Garner was a private man. As far as anyone knows, he never married. He loved to sit in, and he liked to box. He was fond of clothes, and he sampled golf. He had a kind of private language, as he told Art Taylor:

"Who chi coo" is an expression that Sarah Vaughan and I used all the time, years ago . . . We used to hang out together in Atlantic City. It means magnificent obsession. If I dig what you do, what you're playing, you're a magnificent obsession; if I don't, I say nothing . . . People who don't really know me call me Erroll. But Sarah Vaughan, Peggy Lee, and Carmen McRae all know me as "Who chi coo," and that means they love me as much as I love them.

He also told Taylor:

I do a lot of walking, I just go around and watch people; that feeds me and gives me ideas . . . I'm not the type to sleep the day away . . . I like to get out in the daytime and see what others are doing, because they're the same people who come to hear you play the concerts. I like being with people. It feeds me and helps to make my day complete.

Bobby Short knew Garner for a time when Garner lived in Carnegie Hall. "He was always a happy, jolly fellow," Short has said. "He had a nice duplex. He'd wear a head rag around the house, which is the privilege of genius, and he enjoyed being domestic and cooking for himself and his dog. I always liked the answer he gave once when someone mentioned his not being able to read music. He said, 'Hell, man, nobody can hear you read.' "

Super Chops

Some lives pivot on paradox. Dave McKenna has been a jazz pianist thirty years, but it is almost impossible to get him to talk about music beyond, for example, the random observation that there is no such thing as the pure improvisation he constantly practices. He has lived on Cape Cod twelve years, but he has only been in the ocean once. In a society that deifies the automobile, he does not drive. He may be the hardest-swinging jazz pianist of all time, but he lives a quiet, unswinging middle-class life made up largely of eating, playing rumbustious Ping-Pong with his sons, Steven and Douglas, and watching sports on television—particularly the Red Sox, who have been with him all his life. He plays the piano with supreme authority but considers himself a barroom or dance-band pianist. The amplified bass fiddle has become the dominant instrument in jazz during the past decade, but McKenna's left hand is so rhythmically powerful that it brushes the new bassists aside. He is, along with Tommy Flanagan and Jimmy Rowles and Ellis

Larkins, among the best of the post-Tatum pianists, but he
stays low: he is rarely in New York, and in order to hear
him one must travel to Schenectady, the Cape, Rochester,
Boston, Newport.

One night before work at Bradley's he had dinner at An-
tolotti's, on East Forty-ninth Street. He was dolled up in a
three-piece tan corduroy suit, and he ate with his customary
relish—a dozen clams on the half shell, two orders of gnocchi
with marinara sauce, veal piccata, salad, and cheesecake, all
washed down with a couple of Martinis, a white Corvo, a
good Barolo, and espresso. He delivered this brief litany between Martinis: "I'm crazy about Italian cooking, and my
ambition is to eat at every good Italian restaurant in New
York. There must be at least fifty of them. When I was at
Bradley's last year, I went to Gino's, on Lexington at Six-
tieth, and the Amalfi, which moved a while ago from West
Forty-seventh to East Forty-eighth. Tony Bennett hangs
out there when he's in town. I go to Patsy's, on Fifty-sixth
back of Carnegie Hall. Ballato's, down on East Houston, is
great, and Joe's, on Macdougal, is a down-home, peasant-
type place. I come here a lot, and I guess Elston Howard
does, too, because I've seen him twice. I haven't been to
Vesuvio, on West Forty-eighth, for years, but it used to be
fine. I've been to Romeo Salta, and I go to San Marco, on
West Fifty-second. I went recently to San Marino with
Zoot and Louise Sims. I tried Il Monello, at Seventy-sixth
and Second, and Parioli, where Bill Buckley goes. Some
guitarist from Boston told me that Parioli has the best chocolate cake he ever had, which is interesting, because I usually don't go to Italian restaurants for chocolate cake. I'd be
willing to take gigs in New Haven just for the white pizza
they have there. I guess I'd like to be a Craig Claiborne.
That's my idea of putting your heart and your soul into
your work."

He arrived replete at Bradley's, and during his first set,
in which he built a medium head of steam, he fashioned one
of his free-association songfests. He has said that stringing
together songs with common themes helps pass the time

when he is playing. (He also likes to speed up fast numbers, as if he were trying to get them over with as quickly as possible.) He warmed up with "Darn That Dream," "At Sundown," and "When Day Is Done"—which falsely presaged an essay on songs having to do with evening or night, for he abruptly veered into "Silk Stockings" and "Blue Skies." Then came "My Ship," and he had found his text: "Lost in a Fog" was followed by "Red Sails in the Sunset," "On Moonlight Bay," "How Deep Is the Ocean?," "The Devil and the Deep Blue Sea," "Wave," and "I Cover the Waterfront." He closed the set with a beautiful, rocking blues and Zoot Sims' "Red Door."

McKenna sat down at a table near the piano, a fine concert grand left to Bradley Cunningham by the late Paul Desmond. McKenna is a man-mountain, whose perfect proportions contain a massive eagle's head, a logger's forearms, and hot-dog fingers. He is well over six feet, and, possibly for streamlining, he wears his brown hair flat and straight back. When he is at the Cape, he likes to talk about New York and how much he'd love to live there again, and when he is in New York he likes to talk about the Cape. For a while, he spoke with some heat of why the Red Sox had blown the pennant, and when he was asked how the summer had been at the Cape he said, "Good. I like to be around salt water, but the ocean is overstated. Sand is gritty and the ocean has waves. Last year, I went swimming in a freshwater pond, and if I lived near one I'd go in three or four times a day—or would have. Since I've gained weight, I'd never go to a public beach. I'd have to have a private pond."

One afternoon a year or so before that, McKenna, who was stretched out on a beach chair in his back yard in South Yarmouth, talked about his house and his early life. The house is a gray-shingled bungalow and the back yard is largely macadam, from which sprout two basketball nets. A stone barbecue and a picnic table at one edge look un-

used. The surrounding landscape is scrub pine and sand.
McKenna had on a red-flowered sports shirt, worn outside
khaki pants, and sneakers. His chair was surrounded by the
sports pages of the Boston *Globe* and *Herald American*.
"My wife, Frankie, got the house for ten thousand," Mc-
Kenna said. "And we had to borrow a thousand for the
down payment. It only has three small bedrooms. I could
use a music room. It's still fresh air here, but the new houses
are beginning to hem me in. When we moved, it was all
woods. There was nothing next door, and there was nothing behind me. I figured no one would build across the
street between me and Route 6, but they did. The beauty
of being here was all that land to roam in. I'm used to that
from the fields and farms there were around Woonsocket,
Rhode Island, where I was born. I was born there in 1930.
My mother, Catherine Reilly, came from South Boston.
She still plays piano. She studied violin with a member of
the Boston Symphony. She played the top tunes of the time,
but not too forcefully—'Lazybones' and Stormy Weather.'
She's got good ears and knows all the chords and can trans-
pose anything, and she reads better than I do. But I don't
think she ever could have been a dedicated musician. She's
got too much of a sense of humor. My father was from
Woonsocket. He drove a parcel-post truck. He was a street
drummer—that is, he played snare drum in military bands,
like the Sons of Italy—and he also played drums in dance
bands. He had a fantastic roll. His musical likes included
brass bands and the 'William Tell Overture.' But there's
nothing wrong with that. Sousa marches are really put together well, and I've always thought 'The Star-Spangled
Banner' should never be sung but should be played by a
good Sousa or Goldman band. A brass band makes it much
more stirring. My father's father and grandfather had been
drummers before him—his Grandfather McKenna played
drums in the Civil War. I was the first non-drummer in
three or four generations. I have a younger brother, Donald, and two sisters, Jean and Pat. Jean teaches school and
lives with my parents, in Woonsocket, and she's a pretty

good semi-pro singer. She's not a belter and she has good pitch. Pat lives in Barrington, Rhode Island, and is married to a schoolteacher. Woonsocket wasn't a bad place to grow up in. It was a family town, and it was mostly French-Canadian, like all the mill towns in New England. There was semi-professional baseball, and we used to go up to Boston to see the Braves and the Red Sox. I've been a Sox fan since I was seven. I was always more of a fan than a player, although I was in a kind of softball league for a while in New York in the fifties. I played in the outfield, and the team I was with included Zoot Sims and Carl Fontana and Al Cohn, and we played in Central Park. We didn't have a name, and once we beat Jimmy Dorsey's band, which showed up in uniforms. My mother didn't think it was right for her to teach me piano herself, so she sent me to the nuns in parochial school, and they taught me that in-between music with John Thompson music books, and I wasn't interested. But I listened every morning on the radio to 'The 9:20 Club' from Boston, and I heard records by Benny Goodman and Nat Cole and the boogie-woogie pianists. When I was twelve or thirteen, I started playing at showers and weddings, and I joined the musicians' union at fifteen. When I was sixteen, I played with Boots Mussulli around Milford, which was just over the border from us in Massachusetts. Milford was eighty per cent Italian and eighty per cent musicians. That's where I learned about Italian food. There were never any bass players, so I had to finagle around a lot with my left hand to make it sound full, which is why I have that guitar effect—that strumming thing in my left hand now.

"I joined Charlie Ventura's band in 1949. Jackie Cain and Roy Kral had just left, but he still had Ed Shaughnessy on drums and Red Mitchell on bass. I went with Woody Herman's band in 1950, and stayed until I was drafted, in 1951. That was the band that had Conte Candoli and Rolf Ericson and Doug Mettome and Don Fagerquist and Al Cohn and Sonny Igoe. I was a disgraceful, drunken kid, and Woody should have fired me. But the Army solved that. After I was drafted, I tried to connect with a service band, but it didn't work. I took basic training with the M.P.s and I did a lot of K.P., and then they sent me overseas—to Japan, where I went to cooking school, and on to Korea. The Koreans were not allowed to touch any of the food, so we had to do all the cooking. I learned how to bake a cake for a hundred men, and how to make pancakes, but my biscuits were like rocks. I remember the *bong* they made when they landed on the mess tray. I was over there a year and a half. We could hear the artillery all the time, and once we were strafed and I was the last guy left in the cook tent. It was a situation where you pressed yourself so close to the ground your belly button made an imprint. That same time, a fat mess sergeant fainted after he discovered that two .50-calibre bullets passed right through the place he always sat in the tent. There was a service band up the road in Korea, and a drummer from Providence who was in it tried to get me in, but the only opening was for accordion. I'd never played one, so this drummer and another guy borrowed one, and they pumped it while I tried to play, but I couldn't get the hang of it, and I didn't make the band.

"When I got home, Boots Mussulli said I sounded the same, even though I'd hardly touched the piano since I'd been away—which is strange, because I've never had that many chops. My mother desperately begged me to use the G.I. Bill and go to college, but I rejoined Charlie Ventura. I spent the rest of the fifties with Ventura and Gene Krupa and with Stan Getz and a group that Zoot Sims and Al Cohn had. I was with Buddy Rich in 1960. I worked a lot in the sixties with Bobby Hackett and at Eddie Condon's place, in the East Fifties. New York was my headquarters, even though I never had an apartment and lived in hotels. Once in a while, I'd go back to Milford just to eat."

Between 1970 and 1977, McKenna's headquarters were at The Columns, in West Dennis. Housed in a handsome mid-nineteenth-century clapboard building to which huge antebellum columns had been added, it was owned and operated by a gentle, self-effacing man named Warren Maddows, whose great delight was to join McKenna near closing time for a couple of Tony Bennett-inspired songs. (Maddows died in 1978.) At first, McKenna played on a bandstand in the small bar to the left of the front door. It was cluttered and noisy and cheerful, and musicians like Bobby Hackett and Dick Johnson frequently sat in. (Hackett said he considered McKenna "the greatest piano player in the world," and though he was often given to hyperbole, he meant it.) During the summer of 1971, Teddi King sang with McKenna for a month. Zoot Sims and Earl Hines and Teddy Wilson and Joe Venuti and Red Norvo spelled McKenna when he took his rare off-Cape jobs. Maddows never made any money from The Columns, but he often kept it open into the winter, and he gradually expanded it. By the summer of 1977, he had added a spacious yellow-and-white tent to the rear of the building, and late that August he hired Teddy Wilson to play duets with McKenna. One set in the middle of the first week went like this:

McKenna, gleaming in a blue shirt, white pants, and white shoes, sat at a low upright and played "Lover, Come Back to Me," "Dixieland One-Step," "Misty," and "That's a Plenty," and retired. Wilson, in a conservative tie and jacket, effortlessly unreeled "Stompin' at the Savoy," "Tea for Two," "Basin Street Blues," "I Can't Get Started," "Moonglow," and an Ellington medley. McKenna, his face impassive and pleasant, listened to Wilson, and, when Wilson finished, talked about music. McKenna talks rapidly and without preamble. "There was a point in the mid-fifties when I got away from jazz and into listening to songs," he said. "Harold Arlen and Jerome Kern and Alec Wilder. Song-writers are my heroes, and I've always wanted to be one. Take Alec Wilder's 'I'll Be Around.' That's the greatest pop song ever written. I should be learning new songs every day. Instead, I'm playing a lot of the same tunes, and I don't like that. I miss Bobby Hackett; he taught me a lot of tunes. Some pianists can play entire scores, but I can't do

that. I don't think I know *any* of 'My Fair Lady' or any
Leonard Bernstein." When McKenna complains, which he
does a lot, it means he's feeling fine. He said, "I'd have
more fun if I could play just two nights a week. With six
nights, you don't have the enthusiasm. It takes the heat off
you when you play for dancing, which people are happier
doing than just sitting around in their bodies listening. People are always after you to play hot, but I don't have super
chops. I don't know if I play jazz. I don't know if I qualify
as a bona-fide jazz guy. I play barroom piano. I like to stay
close to the melody. When I play, I just tool along, and the
only thing I think about is what I'm going to play next. But
I like to sound even and professional, to keep everything on
an even keel. Very few jazz musicians are complete impro-
visers. The greatest have little patterns they follow. I have
my own patterns, my own licks. Sometimes I play in runs,
because people like to hear those things. Also, I'm getting
paid to do that, so I have to stick them in once in a while.
But I like to deëmphasize them, I like to play more sparingly. I play so many single-note lines because I've listened
more to horn players than to piano players. But I loved Nat
Cole. He came the closest to bending notes on the piano, except maybe Oscar Peterson. I'd rather listen to Nat Cole
than Art Tatum. Tatum makes you sweat too much. I'm
more at home playing alone. I appreciate the coloration of
a bassist, but I'd rather play alone or with a little band. I'd
love to play in a Dixieland band like the one I worked in at
Condon's. 'Whiskey-land jazz,' Hackett called it."

A second upright had been placed akimbo to the first,
and after the intermission Wilson sat down at the piano that
he and McKenna had used and McKenna took the second
one. The two pianists faced one another, and McKenna,
looking as if he were about to play in his first recital, immediately deferred to Wilson, who selected the tunes and
set the tempos. (At the start of the gig, McKenna, in typical knock-himself-down fashion, had expressed fear that he
would not be able to keep up with the fast tempos he knew
Wilson would set.) The first number, "How High the

Moon," was fast, and a pattern was set: Wilson played
the first chorus, McKenna soloed for two choruses, Wilson
soloed, and the two exchanged four-bar breaks before playing the last chorus together. Neither pianist betrays much
emotion when he plays. Wilson, his back straight and his
head tipped slightly forward, occasionally shuts his eyes
briefly and presses his lips together, and McKenna, bent
over the keyboard like a tall person stooping to talk to a
child, wrinkles his brow and evinces a slight gathering of
cheek muscles below his right ear. In recent years, Wilson,
perhaps weary at last of perfecting his exquisite miniaturis-
tic solos, has relied more and more on his patterns, and his
playing has taken on an automatic gentility. McKenna, who
once resembled a controlled Tatum with dashes of Nat Cole
and Wilson, has been going in the opposite direction. His
rhythmic power, spelled out by his ingenious left hand—an
avalanche of guitar chords, ground figures, sharp offbeats,
and pouring single-note melodic lines—has become unfet-
tered. The rock-rock, rock-rock, rock-rock of his time becomes irresistible: it is hypnotic, ecstatic. Nothing remains
still before it. And his right hand has grown more and more
startling. He places his notes so that they jar and sharpen
the beat. He likes to emphasize the first note of a phrase and
then, unexpectedly, the fifth or sixth. He likes to shake up
the listener's rhythmic expectations. He also likes to insert
madcap arpeggios and double-time phrases. It is a joyous,
triumphant, foraging style, and by the end of Wilson and
McKenna's second number it was clear that McKenna was
helplessly blowing Wilson out of the water. Wilson would
effect an almost transparent pointillistic chorus, and then
McKenna, his left hand rolling and rumbling, would roar
into his chorus, and all memory of what Wilson had just
played would be gone. A fast "Who's Sorry Now?" went
by, and the two settled into a long medium blues. Wilson
approaches the blues as if he were nibbling grapes, but Mc-
Kenna shoulders his way in, scattering boogie-woogie basses,
wild stop-time choruses, and thumping low-register explo-
sions in both hands. Wilson remained unperturbed, and the

last number, a short, driving "I'll Remember April," was anticlimactic.

The summer after Maddows' death, McKenna went into the Lobster Boat, several miles down Route 28 toward Hyannis. It has a huge white mock ship's prow that points into a parking lot running along the highway. Behind the prow are a lozenge-shaped lounge and a big, boxy dining room. The lounge has a bar and a small bandstand opposite, which holds an upright piano. The wall back of the bandstand is curved and contains a couple of dozen portholes, each of them fitted out with a hanging plant. The piano bench is flanked by carriage lamps fastened to the wall, and there are candlesticks on the piano and a glass chandelier over it. The ceiling is beamed and decorated with signal flags and ship's wheels, and the patrons sit below in a comfortable rummage shop furnished with sofas, director's chairs, captain's chairs, overstuffed chairs, side tables, and standing lamps. It is three New England parlors placed end to end. A color television set behind the bar was showing a Red Sox-Yankees game, and when McKenna arrived, at eight-twenty, he plunked himself at the bar and watched. Frankie McKenna had driven him over, and she sat at a table next to the piano with a good local Billie Holiday singer named Shirley Carroll. At a quarter to nine, McKenna tore himself away from the television and went into his first set. He had had dinner in Yarmouth Port, in an Italian restaurant called La Cipollina, and had put away a small pizza, chicken piccata, linguine with red clam sauce, a salad, half of Frankie McKenna's shrimps with sweet peppers, and a mocha pudding with whipped cream. He was in a benevolent mood. He began with "Don't Take Your Love from Me," and went on through "The Moon of Manakoora," "Sleepy Lagoon," "Isn't It Romantic," "My Romance," and "My Funny Valentine," ending with a blues, three songs in which Shirley Carroll sat in, and a medium bebop tune. He swung quietly but hard.

He returned immediately to the game, and Frankie Mc-Kenna talked about herself and her life with McKenna. She is short and has shingled gray hair and a soft Carolina accent. She is a pretty woman, with a long-suffering face and a smile that closes her eyes. (McKenna has a tempestuous side, and if he doesn't work it out through his playing or in several banging games of Ping-Pong it is apt to spill over on his family.) "I was born an only child and grew up in North and South Carolina," she said in a gentle voice. "My parents were divorced when I was sixteen. My father, Jimmy Wiggins, was a salesman who could charm the bark off a tree. He was medium-sized and dark-haired and well-mannered—a Southern gentleman. His mother was a McQueen, and derived descent from Mary Queen of Scots. He died several years ago. My mother had long since remarried. She's an attractive lady and a champion bridge player. I went to the University of South Carolina two years on scholarship, and, because I was very poor, took practical courses—secretarial courses. Then I went to New York and lived with a group of Carolina girls who had a large apartment on Riverside Drive. I worked first as a secretary to a sales manager of a lingerie company, but come summer I'd take a leave of absence and go home. I liked being Southern in the North and having an accent, and all that. I also worked for a public-relations outfit and as a secretary at ABC Records. I took little night jobs, too—at Downey's Steak House and Basin Street. I met Dave in 1959 in Junior's Bar & Lounge, a musicians' hangout, and we were married three months later. My mother came up on the plane practically carrying the whole wedding—flowers and all—in her arms. I had a two-room apartment across from London Terrace, on Twenty-fourth, and when Steve, who's eighteen now, was born, it was awful. We moved to a fourth-floor walkup at Ninth and Twenty-first, and Douglas, who's fourteen, was born. I had everything pretty well organized. Summers, I got a portable swimming pool and put it on the roof and filled it from a hose I'd attached to my kitchen sink. Our dog Midge chased a beach ball around the roof and the kids chased her and the people from next door threw pennies in the pool. We came up here the first time in the mid-sixties, and each year we'd buy a junk car and at the end of the summer park it in front of our building and let it die. In the fall of 1966, we decided to move up. It was too much in New York with two small children and Dave's hours and the stairs to walk up. I got to do the moving, because Dave was working, and a man named McCarthy, who lived over us and had offered to help in a weak moment, drove me up in his station wagon. We moved into this house in April of 1967.

"Dave is a complex person. He's honest and he's moral. He doesn't put people down, and he's never squandered money. He's a good father, even though he doesn't take the boys fishing, and all that, and he prefers not to be the disciplinarian. But he's very good in a quiet way when someone gets out of hand. He loves his roots, and he loves house and home. He's the most unmechanical person I've ever seen. I can't stand to watch him when he has a screwdriver in his hand. I have to walk away. But it doesn't matter, because I'm a fixit. That's my therapy. Dave was very, very shy when we were married. His mother told me that he could never accept any kind of compliment when he was growing up. It got him all flustered, and he'd pretend he hadn't heard. But he's getting better, and I think he's beginning to admit to himself that he might be a good piano player."

The Red Sox were leading the Yankees by three runs, and McKenna's second set was effervescent. He played a string of "baby" songs—"Baby Won't You Please Come Home?," "Baby Face," "Melancholy Baby," "Gee, Baby, Ain't I Good to You?," "Oh, Baby," and a stinging, very fast "I Found a New Baby." When he finished, he headed back to the bar, commenting first on how hot it was up on the bandstand and how he wished he could go home and watch the rest of the game in peace.

Good, Careful Melody

Michael Moore is the best jazz bassist alive, and he has appeared at a time when the bass is running amok in jazz. The
instrument has been electrified during the past ten years,
and the old soft, articulate boom-boom-boom has been
replaced by boom-boom-boom. Since most young bassists
either have poor amplifiers or don't know how to use their
amplifiers properly (conditions that still afflict electric guitarists), they produce a tone that is wooden, raucous, and
disquieting. The new bassists have discovered what drummers have long known—that a little manual dexterity (in
the case of bassists, a couple of triplets followed by a good
descending arpeggio and a double-stop) can raise cheers.
This has gone to their heads, and they offer empty, reverberating solos, which are greeted as fulsomely as drum solos
once were. Many of the new bassists have also fallen fash-
ionably under the sway of Indian music. They do not play
their notes on pitch but slide up to them, sometimes over-
shooting and sometimes never arriving at all. This gives

their playing a querulous, singsong quality. Michael Moore balances these aberrations by ignoring them. He concentrates on perfecting his tone, which is rich and even and affecting. He avoids singsong effects and keeps his volume at a gentlemanly level. Most important, he is carrying to new heights the flag of lyricism and melodic beauty borne by all great jazz musicians since the arrival of Louis Armstrong, and he is doing it with a low-pitched stringed instrument that is prone to all manner of tonal difficulties and has a bare three registers. Marian McPartland said recently of Moore, "I first heard him soon after he came to New York from Cincinnati, his home town. In fact, I *hired* him then. He astonished me. He played perfect time, he had pure sound, he chose his notes with great care, and he was quick to learn. He was the best bass soloist I'd ever heard. Most bass solos don't have much content, but his have logic and structure and wholeness. They have such lyricism, such melodic glow, that you don't think of them as bass solos. They are closer to guitar solos, but in the end they're entities unto themselves."

Like all jazz bassists, Michael Moore comes in three parts: the accompanist, the soloist, and the arco player. (Bowing the strings is called arco playing, and plucking them is pizzicato. The pizzicato bass has been brought to a high technical level by jazz players only in the last forty years. At one time, the technique was almost unknown. Hector Berlioz wrote of the Prague Conservatory in the late eighteen-forties, "The study of the violin [and, by extension, the bass violin] is incomplete. Pupils are not taught pizzicato. As a result, a whole host of passages in arpeggios involving all four strings, or in repeated notes with two or three fingers on the same string in rapid tempo—passages that are perfectly feasible, as any guitar player will show you (on the violin)—are said to be impossible and consequently proscribed to composers. No doubt fifty years from now a director with a flair for innovation will take the plunge and lay it down that pizzicato is to be taught in violin classes; and then violinists, having mastered the novel and piquant effects that are possible with this technique, will laugh at

our present-day players.") Bassists and drummers often talk
of hitting the "back" or the "front" of their notes, but
Moore the accompanist hits his in the exact center. He
chooses them according to the situation he finds himself in.
He frequently uses the low notes in the chords of a song,
but in a duo with, say, the guitarist Gene Bertoncini he will
construct countermelodies. When he plays with Teddy
Wilson, he duplicates many of Wilson's left-hand bass
notes. Marian McPartland often piques him, and he wages
exhilarating contrapuntal warfare. But he shies away from
playing with Dave McKenna, feeling that McKenna's left
hand is so strong that he would add little to it. Moore's
solos are models of melodic beauty, of sheer improvisational
exuberance. They surpass the instrument they are played
on. Moore values silence, and he uses it to great effect. He
will start a solo with a rapid descending phrase that begins
in eighth notes and expands into quarter notes. He will
pause, play a triplet, pause again, and repeat the triplet, altering the final note to introduce a falling-and-rising arpeggio delivered with great speed and perfect articulation. He
will pause once more, loose five commanding staccato notes
and go into a series of rapid ascending notes that keep
breaking off. Then still another pause, and he will shoot
into his high register and construct an eight-bar melody
that turns out to be a jubilant new song. After a flurry of
on-the-beat notes, he will close the solo with an unresolved
note, which leaves us with a polite question—"Was it all
right?"—and the promise of more to come. Despite the
headlong quality of Moore's solos, they have a controlled
emotion that takes us right to the heart of his improvisation.
Moore's arco work is regal and delicate and exact. Most jazz
arco playing has a stiff, mahogany sound, and most of it is
off pitch, but Moore stays in tune and has a soft and buoyant tone.

Moore lives with his second wife, the singer Anita Gravine,
in an old slope-shouldered building on Thompson Street, in
SoHo. The apartment is barely big enough to swing a snake

in. It has a cheerful kitchen, dominated by a photograph of Louis Armstrong and a reproduction of Edward Hopper's "Nighthawks." An adjoining bed-sitting-room looks out on an airshaft that occasionally floats a breeze. Off the bed-sitting-room is a narrow room with a window at the end, and leaning against one wall are five basses. The bed-sitting-room has a Victorian rocker, a double bed, a Morris chair, and an unright piano. Moore has half a dozen or so students, each of whom averages a visit a month. A session usually lasts an hour and a half, and is intense and difficult. Moore fills his students until they spill over, for he talks as fast as he can play. He stands most of the time, even when he isn't demonstrating passages on one of his basses. He recently gave a young Canadian bassist, Rick Kilburn (who has worked with Mose Allison and Dave Brubeck), the first lesson he'd had in a few years. Before Kilburn arrived, Moore, pacing the bed-sitting-room, talked about music. He is compact, about six feet all, and has brown hair, and round, gracious Irish-burgher features.

"My main problem with the bass has always been sound," he said, sitting briefly in the rocker and pitching rapidly back and forth. "I have a proper bass sound in my head, but it has taken me years to get near it on my instrument. You should be able to carry that sound from room to room, from tune to tune, without losing it. Jack Teagarden always said, 'Don't let the drummer or anybody else wreck your sound,' and he never did. But trying to perfect that sound first is another matter. I use a Xavier Jacquet bass. It's about a hundred and forty years old. If you had a bass made, it would cost at least six thousand dollars, and it might not be as good, because of the new wood. Old wood is looser and transmits vibrations better. Playing an amplified bass (or raising your strings higher from the board—which most bassists used to do) helps. You don't have to pull the strings so hard just to be heard. At the same time, your sound is apt to become distorted, particularly when you record. Trying to get a natural sound on records—a sound that sounds something like *me*—is driving me crazy, because the young engineers, raised on rock and Fender basses, don't know what a natural bass sound *is*. They feed a wire right into their control panel from my pickup, which would ordinarily be connected to my amplifier. And they put a microphone on my strings, and fiddle with their knobs, and you come out sounding like a tree creaking on a winter night.

"It's easy to forget that the bass player plays just about every beat. A whole band can be ruined by a bad bass player. I've decided that the combination of players in a rhythm section is terribly important. There can be a conflict between two players which will make a rhythm section go. When Miles Davis had Ron Carter and Tony Williams on bass and drums, Carter was the anchor, and Williams tended to rush the beat. That created tension, and tension creates excitement. In John Coltrane's rhythm section, Jimmy Garrison had to be the anchor, too, but for a different reason. Elvin Jones was the drummer, and he has always liked to play off the bass player's time. Elvin has the ability to sound like he's playing *on* the beat when he's playing both the back of the beat *and* the front of the beat. Bass players who work with him have to be very strong. Slam Stewart, who was marvellous thirty-five years ago and is marvellous now, is that strong. He plays right in the center of the beat, and he has the nerves of a thief when he plays way up. Listen to the recording of 'I Got Rhythm' that he and Don Byas did impromptu at a Town Hall concert in the mid-forties. Slam makes himself almost invisible, but the notes are all in the right place. That reminds me of what my father, who's a guitarist, once told me: 'You know the right notes, now learn the best notes.' Bass players should be invisible, instead of sounding as if they were all leaders, which is the way it is now. You have to be unselfish. You have to let the other players take most of the shots. Accompanying different instruments raises different problems. Horn players sound one note at a time, but guitarists might hit four, only one of which will be right for me to play. When I played in a trio with Jim Hall a couple of years ago,

I discovered that he goes in strange harmonic directions, and that even if I chose the correct note it might *sound* wrong, or it might set the tonality going in the wrong direction. Pianists are all different. Teddy Wilson uses all the bass notes in his left hand, so you have to play a lot of the same notes he plays. Modern pianists leave out the bass notes, and that gives you latitude. More and more modern musicians want the sound of the bass right out front, and I hate that. It's an ugly sound. I just got a new amplifier—a Walter Woods. It's made on the Coast, and it's small and very clear and quiet. If I had my way, I'd play without an amplifier. But it isn't possible anymore. Drummers are louder and louder, and, to compensate, the horn players increase their volume and then yell at the bass player to turn up, turn up. If you don't turn up, you can't hear yourself, and it's like going into battle with just a hammer."

Moore, who had been doing figure eights between the kitchen and the bed-sitting-room, sat down on the piano bench. "When I play a good solo, I feel that I've just been sitting by and listening. I think, Where did *that* come from? But if I play badly it's my fault. I've always been attracted to melodic players; nothing else moves me. You have to study a song if you want to improvise on it well. I learn the melody and every note in the chords and the best harmonic way through the tune. Then I'll play the melody straight a couple of times, and sometimes before I perform I'll take a drink to dull the old conscious brain and let the subconcious out. All of which means that you discipline yourself first—because that's what music is: discipline—and then throw the discipline out the window. When I solo, I have a brand-new melody in my head that wants to get out. That's why I leave so many spaces in my solos, why I force myself to wait—so that the melody has the time to get itself organized before it comes out. It's nerve-racking. It's like a ballplayer waiting to swing at the last possible second. But it creates tension in the listener, and then release, and that's what improvising it. You have to keep your intuition open, even if you play a wrong note. Gary Burton told me once that there is no note that can't be fixed, and he's right. A good improviser should study good songs. They fill his head with melody, and eventually all that melody will come out in a new form. I see the bass in a strange way. The tone is the same as melody: they get mixed up together. They become indivisible. Of course, I hear things in my head that I can't play—that are perhaps impossible to play on any instrument. But complexity has nothing to do with beauty. You don't have to sound like Coltrane on the bass, which is what most of the young players are trying to do. The bass by nature is closer to the spaced-out playing of Miles Davis and Lester Young. It is also a lower-register instrument, and many bassists forget that. They forget that people don't hear notes down there as easily as they do the higher notes. Pure technique will go right by the listener's ear, whereas good, careful melody will rest in it."

Kilburn turned out to be thin, dark-haired, and relaxed. Moore gave him a bass and stationed him near the kitchen door. He put a book of bass exercises on a music stand. The exercises were by Ludwig Streicher, the Austrian master basist, whose new methods of fingering and bowing have become a passion for Moore. The Streicher bowing method involves rotating the bow from one side of the hair to the other when crossing strings, to make a smooth, connected sound. The thumb lies lightly over the top of the bow shaft and the little finger on the bottom of the frog. The little finger becomes the bow's rudder. Streicher suggests dropping the left elbow from a horizontal position, so that it points more toward the floor. This eliminates the pain in the arms and sides that bassists often experience after a half hour of playing. He also suggests that bassists stop draping themselves over their instrument. Keeping the left foot cocked against the bottom of the bass's sound box helps in pulling back on the instrument, provided the peg that the bass rests on isn't too long. Moore taught Streicher's methods by demonstration, and Kilburn slowly bent himself to the new ways. Moore told him to go through Streicher's book several times—the new methods would soon fall into place, and he'd have trouble remembering the old ones. Then Moore abruptly sat down at the piano and played a medium-tempo version of "What Is This Thing Called Love?" He played chords hooked together by spindly runs, and Kilburn accompanied him pizzicato, Kilburn soloed, and when they had finished Moore gave him an extended reading, on harmony and scales, which became increasingly abstruse but began this way:

"What are you thinking about in the first part of that tune? What harmonic decisions can you make?"

"A C-sharp diminished scale?" Kilburn said.

"That's one you can use. But there are other possibilities: the C whole-tone scale or the D-flat melodic minor scale."

On the piano, Moore played some of the scales he recommended, and he played some on the bass, his fingers moving like hummingbirds up and down the strings, his tone filling the room.

Kilburn watched intently. When Moore's lecture on harmony was almost over, Kilburn asked, "How do you think of all these things when you're playing? Do you know them well enough to do them without thinking about them?"

"Yes," Moore said. "Unless the song is new. Then I woodshed first."

"When I have to play a new tune, I learn the chords, but I depend more on my intuition, and what I do often sounds wrong to me."

Moore nodded. "The intellect has to train your ear. You have to feed new information into the computer, and practice that information intellectually. Then, when that information becomes intuitional to your ear, the melody will flow out."

"I'm an ear player, but eighty per cent of the time I can sound like I'm not."

"Most bass players are boring, because they think from the bottom of their instrument to the top rather than from the top down. Streicher's methods make it easier to think from the top. Anyway, you should learn to be a good team player first, like Ron Carter, and worry about soloing last of all. The bass is especially difficult, because the notes aren't right there in front of you. Half of playing the instrument is finding the notes, and half is making them come out clearly and well—particularly the low ones, which tend to run together."

"I've got to clarify all this, and it will take time," Kilburn said.

"That's right. It will. But nothing to worry about."

Kilburn's lesson lasted a couple of hours. When he had left, Moore sat down again in the rocker and drank a beer. He talked for a while of how promising he thought Kilburn was. Then, reminded of beginnings, he talked of his own.

"I started on accordion in third grade in Cincinnati. I took lessons with a friend of my father's for three years, and he never knew I couldn't read music. I won ten dollars in a talent show for playing 'After You've Gone' in block chords that my father had taught me, and I won simply because I kept going. Then I was out of school a year with nephritis, and that was the end of the accordion. In junior high school, I was told to pick an instrument for the school band that the school would buy, and I chose the tuba. I hated it. I went to Withrow High School, and they needed a bass player for the school jazz band, so I switched then and there. My father bought me a Kay plywood bass, and I studied with Dave Horine. He'd played with my father, and he had a bass shop. I was easily discouraged. When I tried to use a bow the first time, it sounded so bad to me I didn't play at all for months. I studied with Harold Roberts, who was a symponic bassist. And I became a part of the Withrow Minstrels, a high-calibre musical organization run by George Smith, who was the musical director and something of a legend in Cincinnati. Smith would hire professionals when he needed them for his shows, which were practically Paul Whiteman productions. In fact, he used my father in his very first one.

"I graduated from high school in 1963, and played at the

Playboy Club in Cincinnati with a pianist named Woody
Evans, then with the guitarist Cal Collins. He was a natural
player, but he wasn't much help when you asked him what
such-and-such a chord was. He'd say, 'Oh, that's kind of an
E chord.' The Cincinnati College Conservatory of Music
took me on scholarship for a year. Then Dee Felice, a local
drummer, recommended me to Nat Pierce, who was Woody
Herman's pianist, and I joined Woody the day after Christmas in 1966. That was the band that had Marvin Stamm and
Ronnie Zito and Bill Chase and Frank Vicari and Sal Nistico
and Carl Fontana. They'd had a bunch of bass players with
bad beats. I couldn't read well, but I knew how to keep time,
so I worked out. But I worked out in spite of myself. I was
a pretty testy kid. I hadn't been in the band two weeks
when I had my first scene with Woody. He's an old-time
bandleader who not only knows how to handle a band but
knows how to handle audiences as well. He's tough and he's
savvy. Scott La Faro was my big influence, and I had all
these notions that I was going to free the bass, so during a
performance I started accompanying just the saxophones,
ignoring the rest of the band. Of course, it was crazy, because the bass player is supposed to anchor the whole band.
Then I took a girl on the bus without saying anything to
anybody, and *that* bugged Woody. I didn't understand the
hierarchy in a big band—that if Stamm or Chase wanted to
take a girl on the bus, O.K. They had long since proved
themselves. But if a new player like me wanted to, he had to
introduce the girl to Woody, just as if he were bringing her
home to his family. We had another blowup in Morocco.
'Satin Doll' was the bass feature, and during it Woody
would hold the mike on the bass. But halfway through my
solo he leaned over and said, 'Watch your intonation, pal.'
That did it. Afterward, I picked him up and swung him
around and told him he better get another bass player, and
left the band. But later I went back and subbed with the
band. After all the scenes, you become part of the family.

"I studied two more years in Cincinnati, with Frank Proto,
and came to New York in 1968. I worked right off with

Marian McPartland. She's always open to new players and new tunes, and she plays better and better and better. You can use confidence when you first come to this town, and she built it up. I was with Marian a year, and with Freddie Hubbard for a while, and then with Jimmy Raney. Then I moved back to Cincinnati. I was married and we had a mongoloid child, and things weren't working out well with him in New York. In Cincinnati, I spent a lot of time with older retarded kids, just to see how they functioned, what they were like. They were often slow and lazy, but my son wasn't. We found that he was educable, and now he talks a mile a minute, and he reads. He's sharp and he's got all the human qualities, and sometimes they get in the way. I wish I could see more of him and be closer to him. My wife and I were divorced, and I only see him twice a year. After nine months in Cincinnati, I missed New York so bad I came back, and joined the Ruby Braff-George Barnes Quartet. It was tightly structured and had an immediately identifiable sound. None of the solos were long, and we communicated with audiences on both a traditional and a modern level. Barnes was a great guitarist in his older, chunky way. He was totally ordered and never wasted a note. I'd be amazed at the sounds he'd get off sometimes. He even sounded like a clarinettist once in a while. It was too bad, but a venom developed between the two men after a time. Ruby is the most honest guy I have ever known. He just doesn't know how to smile and say O.K. He *has* to say what he thinks, no matter the grief. But he's a super player and we're good friends. I go up to his place in Riverdale, and he plays me all sorts of Louis Armstrong tapes and tells me wild Sid Catlett stories."

Moore stood up and stretched, and sat down on a stool that Kilburn had used in his lesson. "I was born in a suburb of Cincinnati—Glen Este—in 1945. I'm an only child. My father's sixty-one now, and he has white hair and a white beard. He's not too tall, and he has a great sense of humor. He's a kind of Cincinnati Ruby Braff who always says the wrong thing. He's a really fine guitarist, Charlie Christian style. For years, in the forties and early fifties, he had a Nat Cole-type trio with a piano player named Teddy Raeckel. They were busy until the bottom dropped out in the mid-fifties. My father went into the insurance business, and he was very unhappy. But now he's retired and back in music. He practices several hours a day and works three or four nights a week. He used to dress Brooks Brothers style, but now he's looser, with his beard and all. He sat in with Marian McPartland one night, and she tried to hire him, but he wouldn't do it. My mother's an elegant, white-haired, tall lady who's very composed, very self-contained. She knows herself and is comfortable with what she knows. She came from Ripley, Ohio, and her maiden name was Jean-nette Gardner. She has an autobiography written by my great-great-great-grandfather, who was a circuit preacher. He published church music and travelled by flatboat down the Ohio River in 1810. And he cleared the land and fought bears and mountain lions. *His* father fought in the Revolu-tion. There have been a lot of musicians in my family. One of my grandfathers had a country band, and an uncle played bass. My mother taught piano fourteen years. She plays very well, and although she never could have been a performer, I think she sold herself short. She used to try to teach my Dad to read music, but he was scared to death of it. I in-herited the feeling. I can read, but it makes me nervous. A couple of years ago, I sent my parents to Europe on a tour. They'd hardly ever been out of Ohio. At first, my father was Mr. World-wise—'I don't want to travel with a bunch of tourists,' and all that. But he bought the Eiffel Tower and everything else he saw in Paris and Rome and Venice and London. When they got back, they looked more alive and happy than I'd ever seen them. They'd bailed me out a number of times, and I figured it was a good thing for me to do."

Ten Levels

Like most revolutions, bebop, which flourished from the mid-forties to the mid-fifties, eventually dressed up in new clothes most of the traditions that it had set out to change or destroy. It broadened the harmonic base of swing with augmented chords, and everybody sounded as if he were playing "wrong" notes. But in the process bebop musicians constructed a stout harmonic cage and locked themselves in it. It became fashionable to play all the notes in these expanded chords—to "run the changes"—and the result was a Niagara prolixity. All that mattered was how many eighth or sixteenth notes you could play in a thirty-two- or sixty-four-bar solo. Bebop tried to free jazz rhythmically. Drummers shifted the main beat to their big ride cymbals, and used their bass drums and snare drums for accents that became a dense rhythmic rain. Horn players and pianists and guitarists were soaked by snare-drum triplets and offbeats and by bass-drum "bombs." These rhythmic decorations

gave the music a nervous, addled air. Bebop drummers tightened and constricted the easy ocean motions of the great
swing drummers, like Jo Jones and Sidney Catlett. Bebop
drummers chattered but didn't talk, droned but didn't sing.
For all the accidental limitations of bebop, its finest practitioners were endlessly inventive. Charlie Parker was their
champion. He was the supreme jazz improviser. His ballad
playing suggested a new kind of legato music, a music of
unparalleled melodic intensity, and his blues playing, though
full of the old verities, revealed new depths of feeling.

All bebop players were influenced by Parker, but the
alto saxophonist Lee Konitz absorbed his Parker in careful
doses. In the beginning, he listened to Benny Carter and
Johnny Hodges and Pete Brown, and after that to Lester
Young. His first recorded solo, on Gil Evans' arrangement
of Parker's "Anthropology," done by Claude Thronhill's
big band in 1947, is a sliding, angular blend of Carter and
Young, with Carter's peculiar step phrasing and Young's
aluminum tone. Young took over increasingly in the early
fifties (the late Paul Desmond listened to Konitz in this
period); then streaks of Parker began to show. "I started
listening to Charlie Parker records in the late forties,"
Konitz has said, "but he was too strong for me. It took me
at least a year to hear him. People said then that Lee Konitz
was the only young alto player around who didn't sound
like Charlie Parker. Well, later Lee Konitz did sound like
Charlie Parker. I often tell my students to learn this or
that Charlie Parker solo. He created our études, and to learn
a Charlie Parker solo can change your life."

Lester Young's sound and his horizontal attack and
Parker's fluidity and bite can still be heard at the back of
Konitz' playing, but his style is his own. It has great gentle-
ness and subtlety. At one time, he and Paul Desmond
sounded almost identical. Desmond never changed: his tone
remained perfumed and ivory. Konitz' sound has taken on
weight and authority. He has always been free of clichés.
He surprises you no matter how many times you hear him
play "All the Things You Are" and "You Go to My Head"

and "These Foolish Things." His attack is a shrewd mixture of short phrases, often compounded of repeated notes, and long horizontal utterances capped by his barely perceptible vibrato. His solos are full of secrets. Clear, boldface passages are followed by shadowy turns, made up of half a dozen ascending notes or of quick bent notes or of skidding Charlie Parker runs. These mysterious, always soft insertions give the impression that he is talking in two voices at once—to us and to himself. It is as if he were continually cautioning himself. Konitz likes silence, and sometimes at the start of a set he will play a short phrase, repeat it, and fall silent for two or three measures. He may start a new idea, discard it, and fall silent again. He is an excellent slow-ballad player, who savors the melody, lingering over a note here, eliminating a note there, but never getting in the composer's way. He has in recent years taken up the soprano saxophone, and he plays it with a bright, piping sound but without the rotund Bechet authority. Konitz played the tenor saxophone before the alto, and once in a while he goes back to it. He even recorded on it with Jimmy Rowles and Michael Moore. His playing sounded slow and muffled, as if the tone of the instrument were simply too heavy for a nimble alto saxophonist to move around. Konitz will try anything. During the seventies, he recorded with traditional bebop groups, with his own nine-piece band, in a jam-session setting, in duos, with free-jazz groups, and, stepping onto Olympus, all by himself.

Konitz got off to a unique start. Between 1947 and 1953, he recorded with four groups that were among the most eccentric and/or modern outposts in jazz: Claude Thornhill, the Miles Davis nonet, Lennie Tristano's sextet, and Stan Kenton. He had a rare talent for being in the odd place at the right time. Thornhill was an easygoing pianist and arranger who had done studio work, led his own groups, and recorded with Bunny Berigan, Benny Goodman, and Billie Holiday. This Thornhill band, put together in 1946, lasted about three years, and there was no other dance band like it. Gil Evans did many of its arrangements, and his scores

called for an instrumentation of three trumpets, two trom-
bones, two horns, tuba, clarinet, alto saxophone, two tenor
saxophones, baritone saxophone, and piano, guitar, bass, and
drums. Evans had already found his swanlike sound. Poised
somewhere between Debussy and Duke Ellington, it converted a dance band into a Turner sunset. "I joined Thornhill in Chicago, and I stayed with him ten months," Konitz
has said. "It was my first big-time situation. I was nervous
and impetuous, and I had wise-guy tendencies, like wearing
brown suède shoes and yellow socks with a tuxedo. A lot of
the musicians—like Billy Exiner, the drummer, and Danny
Polo, the clarinettist, and Barry Galbraith, the guitarist—
were older, so I thought I was hipper, when actually they
were hipper than I was. Danny Polo was a great influence.
He cooled me off, and I had to learn. I gave up pot a while
ago, but I had started smoking in that band. I guess it was a
tranquillizing factor. So much so that one night when I
walked out to the microphone to solo I simply stood there
and dug Exiner and Galbraith and the bassist Joe Shulman,
who were cooking like the Basie rhythm section. I stood
there and listened for a chorus and then walked back to my
seat without playing a note. It was a ballad band with a luxurious instrumentation, and Gil Evans gave it an extraordi-
nary tonal palette. He also taught the band how to phrase
bebop. It's a very specific discipline, and I'm still working
at it. A lot of musicians avoided its difficulties and went on
tangents. I believe Ornette Coleman was one. I don't believe
he ever quite learned his Charlie Parker before he took off
on his own. Thornhill himself was a shy man, and all our
contacts were good-natured. I suspect the music was a little
ahead of him. Gil Evans and I keep in touch, and we have
even worked as a duo. In the late seventies, we went to Italy
and played concerts. One was in Potenza, in the south. I
think it was the first itme they'd heard a jazz concert, or
maybe even jazz. They were polite, but they couldn't quite
sit still. So I walked out into the audience and played, and I
could feel Gil back at the piano opening one eye to see
where the hell I'd gone. But it worked and they loved it. It

was hard, just the two of us. Gil went out bloody every
night, but he always felt like doing it again the next night."

Konitz' next recording adventures involved the famous
Miles Davis "Birth of the Cool" sessions for Capitol Records, in 1949 and 1950, and Konitz' first sessions with the
blind pianist and teacher Lennie Tristano, in 1949. The Davis records grew directly out of Evans' Thornhill arrangements. They also grew out of the commingling in Evans'
West Fifty-fifth Street basement salon of Konitz and other
Thornhill alumni and such young movers and shakers as
John Carisi, Gerry Mulligan, John Lewis, Max Roach, and
Davis. The nonet was made up of trumpet, trombone, horn,
tuba, alto saxophone, baritone saxophone, piano, bass, and
drums. It had one or two brief gigs in New York, recorded
twelve numbers, and disbanded. Evans arranged two num-
bers ("Boplicity," "Moon Dreams"), Mulligan five ("God-
child," "Venus de Milo," "Rocker," "Jeru," "Darn That
Dream"), Carisi one ("Israel"), Lewis three ("Move,"
"Budo," "Rouge"), and Davis one ("Deception"). Davis,
Mulligan, Konitz, and Thornhill's tubist, Bill Barber, were
on all the numbers; Roach and Kenny Clarke, Lewis and Al
Haig, and J. J. Johnson and Kai Winding alternated. The
Capitol nonet is the Thornhill band in miniature. It seethes
with harmony and indirect melody. Sounds die away, and
reënter by the side door. No voice is raised, and the soloists
are less important than the ensembles. It is a curled, begloved
music, and the principal effect it had on jazz was the West
Coast movement of the fifties—a pale, swinging white small-
band jazz that eventually faded away when its main players
went into the studios. Konitz' part in the nonet was largely
decorative, although he had several brief solos. He once
told Ira Gitler, "As much as I enjoyed sitting there and
playing with the band and as lucky as I was to get a couple
of good licks on the records, I felt I wasn't as completely
involved as I would like to have been. If it existed again, I
would enjoy it that much more because I would know what
a musical potential there was."

In 1980, Konitz was given another chance, and he recently explained how it happened: "Martin Williams, at the Smithsonian, asked if the nine-piece group I had had in the seventies could re-create the old Miles Davis 'Cool' records, and I said we could. He wanted us to play the material at a couple of concerts in Washington. I didn't know where the arrangements were, so I called Miles. I hadn't had any communication with him in years, and he wasn't interested. He didn't want to hear about it. I told Martin we might have to transcribe the recordings. I started listening, but there were lots of passages in the ensembles I simply couldn't decipher. Like in 'Godchild,' which was written by George Wallington and arranged by Gerry Mulligan, who had been the aggressive force behind the Capitol dates. I called up Gerry and went out to his house in Connecticut. We played the record, and he couldn't hear it, either. So he rewrote 'Godchild'—in four hours. It was just wonderful to see him work. And he rewrote 'Jeru' and 'Rocker,' too. Beautiful-looking scores, with delicate, spidery notation sprouting on the paper. Johnny Carisi had his score of 'Israel,' and John Lewis helped me sketch out 'Move,' although he wasn't as interested as Mulligan. When I'd taken all the arrangements to the copyist, I called Miles, because I was on my way to Pittsburgh to do a school clinic on cool jazz and I wanted to know if he had any words for the kiddies. He had a quick response: 'I don't give a ——— what you tell them,' in that guttural way he has of talking. So I said, 'Miles, remember my asking you for the arrangements to the "Cool" sessions? Well, we've transcribed them and rewritten them and put them together again.' He said, 'Man, you should have asked me. Those ——— are all in my basement.' I told Gil Evans about the conversation, and he said, 'Miles wouldn't have told you he had everything in the basement if you hadn't first told him you'd gone to the trouble to transcribe the records.' Miles is a bona-fide eccentric."

Konitz had met Lennie Tristano in Chicago in the early forties, and he was not to be free of him for twenty years. Tristano died in 1978, at the age of fifty-nine. He was a mysterious, autocratic semi-recluse who attracted disciples and cultivated his own messianic tendencies. He rarely

played in public, and he made relatively few records. His
energy went into teaching—in a studio on East Thirty-
second Street and in a house in Queens. He was an exceptional Art Tatum pianist who liked to experiment with
tricky time signatures (5/4 or 3/8 against a steady 4/4),
with shifting keys, and with free improvisation. His 1949
recordings "Intuition" and "Digression" preceded the first
official free-jazz efforts by at least a dozen years. His rest-
less single-note melodic lines can be heard sometimes in
Dave McKenna and in the work of the late Eddie Costa, but
his influence has never been wide. "I first heard Lennie
Tristano in Chicago when I was fifteen or sixteen," Konitz
once said. "I was with Emil Flint, and I heard Tristano playing with a Mexican rumba band. I could hear all these fantastic locked-hands chords over the music. I sat in, and he
didn't say anything. Years later, in an interview, he said I
had sounded rotten. Anyway, I asked him if we could get
together, and I started studying with him. We eventually
worked together in some of the Chicago cocktail lounges.
You can trace Lennie Tristano through Roy Eldridge and
Lester Young and Charlie Parker and Art Tatum and Earl
Hines and Nat Cole and also through Paul Hindemith and
Bartók and Bach. He was already doing what he became famous for—the long, long melodic lines, the counterpoint,
the continually changing time signatures. It was fast company for me, and I always felt in way over my head. In
fact, I still don't feel I've mastered Tristano's discipline. His
dedication to his music was infectious, and he changed
everyone who came in contact with him. He was at his
best when he was teaching and playing. Otherwise, he got
stranger and stranger. He generally refused to play in public after the fifties, and he took to staying in his pajamas all
day. Once you were a part of Tristano's school, you were
regarded as a traitor if you left, as I was when I joined Stan
Kenton in 1952, even though I needed the work. I left
Tristano for good in 1964, and we never communicated
again. He had a big old house in Queens in the late fifties,
and I lived there two years. I remember sitting on a glassed-in
porch and reading 'War and Peace' and feeling like some

kind of landowner, while everything around me was actually like a loony bin.

"I studied with Lennie four or five years in all. It's hard to say exactly what I learned. I mean, you learn the major scales, the minor scales, the triads, but beyond that it's the things you talk about when you're not playing or studying. I once asked him about a large concern of mine, which was to eliminate what was making me play mechanically at the time. 'The hippest thing you can do is not play at all,' he said. 'Just listen.' Since then, I have been very concerned about not playing unless it means something. 'Are you contributing?' I keep asking myself. 'Are you a vital part of the situation?' "

Konitz has little to say of his time in Stan Kenton's huge, gleaming Art Deco band. "Conte Candoli and Richie Kamuca and Sal Salvador and Frank Rosolino and Bill Russo were in that band," Konitz has said. "It had ten brass, and the reeds served mainly as padding. Every once in a while, one of the saxophonists would remove the reed, take the neck off his horn, and look deep into the bell to see if he could find a way to make more noise, to be heard better. But Kenton—that great giant of a man—was always very pleasant to work for. I left the band in 1954. I had married in 1947, and I had five kids. I moved out to Long Island and worked as a single and taught and tried to raise my family, and things were rough for me.' "

Konitz is a short, rounded man with scholarly hands and small feet. He has a helmet of curly hair, he affects aviator glasses, and his face is longer than it looks. His close-set eyes resemble headlights on a small car. He likes to talk in bursts, which he punctuates with whistles, *phews*, and polite Bronx cheers. An autobiographical paragraph might sound like this:

"I was born in Chicago October 13, 1927. I grew up on the North Side, in the Rogers Park area. I had two brothers, who were six and nine years older. My father, Abe, was in the dry-cleaning business, and he was good-natured, and I think of myself as being like that. I have a recollection of

him working *all* the time [whistles]. We never starved, but
it was hard going, and sometimes we lived in rooms behind
the shop. My father was born in Poland, and my mother in
Russia. She was five feet tall, but she was the strong one
[*phew*]. I was the outsider in the family. I was light, and
everyone else was dark. I was musical, and they weren't. I
was, as the joke went, the milkman's son. I became a sort of
prima donna early, and they went along with it. When I
wanted a clarinet, which I took up at eleven, they got me
one. I studied four years, mostly with Lou Honig, who's
still teaching [*phhht*]. I've often thought I'd like to take
all those lessons over again, because there were so many
things that I misunderstood, like proper breathing. I thought
for years that I had air going directly into my stomach
[whistles]. I played with a little band in grammar school,
and I played Ravel's 'Boléro' in a recital—just with a drummer. I played with a dance band in high school, and I sang
Tex Beneke vocals and things like ' 'Round the Clock
Blues'—this little Jewish kid with horn-rims singing black
blues [*phew*]. When I was seventeen, I replaced Charlie
Ventura in Teddy Powell's band. Then I went with Jerry
Wald, and took up alto saxophone, but Wald never let me
take any solos, which was just as well because improvisation was still a mystery to me [whistles]."

Konitz talked about his playing: "Joe Dixon, the clarinettist and teacher, told me once, 'You sound like you're
not thinking when you're soloing,' and he's right. He has a
scientific attitude, and he puts these melodies together he's
worked out. But I don't have a surefire musical vocabulary.
I'm riveted to where I am when I play—to the people
around me. I hear everything the piano and bass and drums
are doing, and I lay the right notes on them, and each of
those notes has to affect the following one. It's a lovely experience when it works out with a rhythm section. It's
reaching out and touching one another. It's a nice place to
be, and you can go anywhere from there.

"I think of improvisation as coming in ten levels, each
one more intense than the one before. On the first level,
you play the melody, and you should sound as if you were

playing it for the very first time. Freshly. If it doesn't sound that way, you're not ready to go to the second level. Playing the melody properly gives you the license to vary it, to embellish it, which is what you do on the second level. The melody is still foremost, but you add little things to it on the third level. Variation—displacing certain notes in the melody—comes in around the fourth level, and by the time you get to five, six, and seven you are more than halfway to creating a new song. Eight, nine, and ten are just that—the creation of wholly new melodies. Moving through these ten levels can take place during a set or over the course of an evening. Sometimes, though, you never get past three or four or five, but that's O.K., because no one level is more important than any other.

"When things got bad in the sixties, I still had little gigs and I always practiced, so I never felt I was falling behind. In the seventies, I married my second wife, Tavia. I worked a lot at Stryker's, which was just down the street from where I live, on West Eighty-sixth. And I worked a lot at Gregory's, on the East Side. Then a man from Italy asked me if I would put together nine bodies for a group. The idea appealed to me, and I got advice and some arrangements, and we played off and on at Stryker's and in Europe. We also play at the Village Vanguard a couple of times a year. I'm middle-aged, but I'm still tooting on my tooter, and I see no end to it. It's still a severe challenge—never a cup of tea. It's some sort of gift to me, and I feel very fortunate to be able to earn my bread doing it. I have plans of really getting active. I'm learning to play the piano. The last few years, I've had some degree of solvency. It begins to seem possible to rent a studio. As I see it, I'll play as long as I feel good and then become an artist-in-residence. You get to the point where you have to start listening to younger players, and that's difficult. I took a couple of piano lessons from Harold Danko, who has worked for me, so am I going to be afraid he'll talk around—'Hey, Lee Konitz studied with *me*'? You have to keep playing with younger people. I hate to deny being moved by something new."

Ornette

Few twentieth-century innovators have got in their own way as often as Ornette Coleman, the composer, saxophonist, trumpeter, and violinist. When Coleman opened with his quartet—Don Cherry on pocket trumpet, Coleman on plastic alto saxophone, Charlie Haden on bass, Billy Higgins on drums—at the original Five Spot, on Cooper Square, in the fall of 1959, he became an immediate sensation, and he split the hip New York musical community in two. His detractors (John Hammond, Miles Davis, Charles Mingus) said he was a charlatan and a bore, and his admirers (Gunther Schuller, Martin Williams, Leonard Bernstein) said he was a genius who would forever alter improvisatory music. But by 1962 Coleman, who had come from almost complete obscurity in California, had dropped out of sight, and he has reappeared only rarely. He has worked about ten times in New York night clubs since then, and he has given roughly the same number of concerts. His recording career has been equally fitful. He issued nothing between 1961 and

1965, and very little between 1969 and 1975; only a handful of records have appeared since. He is a stubborn and brilliant visionary and a man of great integrity, and, paradoxically, these attributes have hobbled him. He quickly decided that many New York club owners and recording executives were greedy, shortsighted, racist, and tin-eared, and that they were not willing to pay him what he had been led to believe he was worth. (He once said, "Being poor is not because money doesn't exist and being rich doesn't mean you know everything. But in America art has more to do with the reproductions and selling than with the art itself. That's one reason why musicians are crazy and painters are crazy when it comes to what they think they're worth.") Coleman countered this seeming mean-mindedness by asking for phenomenal sums for night-club dates and recording sessions, and when he was turned down he shrugged and went underground. Coleman talks and writes the way he plays. He uses straightforward English words, but he arranges them in unique, sometimes incomprehensible ways. He has invented his own R. P. Blackmur language, and it is abstract, aphoristic, poetic, philosophical, comic, and nonsensical. Coleman once gave an interview to the jazz critic Leonard Feather, and in it he said:

> In America you can know exactly who you would like to pattern yourself after and what you'd like to do, but the moment you find something you can do that outdates that—or even to make it better, so to speak—it's no longer the same idea anymore, it's a different thing. And every person that challenges the heart of modern expression is going to come up with that problem. I guess it must be a healthy problem. It could be even more healthy if a solution could be made where every person could express his consciousness to its fullest without outdating the particular information he's gotten to do that—or to enhance it. The world would be ten times more productive.

He wrote these liner notes for his "Body Meta" album:

> What you should never know is to never find out you shouldn't.

If you can read or write and you don't write or read why?
What face would you like for a race other than your own
we all don't care if its on money when their is no food
home job and no one cares.
Systems are number by system to provide us a chance to
change them during one's own life time.
Death wealth knowledge poverty are all you got to change
not the people.
No army wears a different uniform.
A woman loves from within and without news, heard,
printed, she is called mother.
The most emotional separation is done by the mating of the
genders.
Fear of fears in the ears eyes lies dead in the head from unknown strangers.
Their are endless ways to take but their is only one way to
give and that is in person.
The pop. of the earth will never be at the same place at the
same time so what do we mean when say the end of
the world?
Body Meta.

Coleman talks about his life more clearly than he talks
about his philosophy or his music. (He has written an un-
published book of musical theory, of which his friend John
Snyder, who is a lawyer, record producer, and former
trumpet player, has said, "I've worked on the manuscript
for hours, for days, with Ornette, but it just doesn't read.
The pages won't follow.") He doesn't like to dwell on his
early days. He was raised in poverty, and his iconoclasm,
which crystallized in his teens, brought him abuse and pain.
He has said of those days, "I was born March 9, 1930, in
Fort Worth, Texas, which is about thirty miles from Dallas.
I grew up with my mother, Rosa, who died in 1976, and
my sister Truvenza, who lives in Fort Worth and is a
singer. My other sister was killed in an automobile accident
when she was seventeen. My father's name was Randolph.
He died when I was seven. I remember sitting on his lap.
He was tall and very dark. I've heard since that he could
sing and that he played baseball. Also that he was a con-
struction worker and a cook. My father and mother were

both born on December 25th, and I think they were from
Hearne, Texas. My mother was tall and dark and very
strict. She was religious-like, and she didn't smoke or drink
or go to night clubs or movies. She only heard me play
once—in a concert in 1966—and whenever I went home
there would be the records of mine I had sent her, un-
opened. She'd say, 'Your records are here.' I think she did
something like selling Avon products, because I recall my
sister taking me to a black woman's house in the ghetto. She
had a school in her house, and I played with blocks. I was
about two, and it cost twenty-five cents a day. But often we
didn't have any money, and I'd go without food.

"I went to two different schools—both black, and both
very good and strict. A teacher spanked me once because I
told her she was wrong. But I was right, and I believe that
to this day. I learned quickly in school that all you had to
know was the answers. I also learned that once you found
out what you should know you didn't have to be there
every day. I had to walk about three miles over a lot of
train tracks to my first school, and I'd get tired, and some
days I'd never make it. When my mother found out, she
near beat me to death. I used to dream of being an adult.
I'd see myself as an adult, but I could never see *what* I
would be. In high school, I played football, and I liked running. I got my collarbone broke playing football, and it
took a long time to heal. When I was in the eleventh grade,
my mother bought me an alto saxophone with money I had
saved. I taught myself to read, and joined a church band of
twenty or twenty-five people. We went to different churches
in Texas, and played for conventions. It was a marching
band, an "Onward, Christian Soldiers' band. The only other
music I knew about was rhythm and blues. So I was amazed
when I heard Lester Young at a jam session in Fort Worth.
They were playing show tunes, and they all had this 'bridge'
in the middle, which the blues didn't have. So I set out to
learn popular songs. But to make a living you had to play
rhythm and blues. I got a tenor saxophone and played R. &
B., doing all that leaning backward and jumping on table-

tops, and that sort of showmanship. I had my own band when I was seventeen. I copied things off the radio, off records. I learned the white repertory, the Mexican repertory, the black repertory. White people liked 'Star Dust,' black people liked 'Flyin' Home.' I would buy sheet music and teach songs to the band. We learned things like Pete Johnson's recording of '627 Stomp.' The alto solo on that first made me want to play the saxophone. One of the people in my band was an alto player named Ben Martin. I liked him better than Charlie Parker. He could play very, very beautiful. He made me cry like a baby, he was so beautiful. He was a cross between Jimmy Dorsey and Charlie Parker.

"I graduated from high school in the late forties, and I got offers for scholarships to black colleges. I went to one meeting at Samuel Huston College, in Austin, but they were too snobby for me, even though I'd heard they had a very good band. I was already supporting my mother and sister, making a hundred dollars a week. Then a minstrel show, 'Silas Green from New Orleans,' came through Fort Worth, and I auditioned and got a job. I told my mother I was going to Dallas. We ended up in Natchez, where I got fired. Then I went to New Orleans and on to Baton Rouge. I guess I looked like a Christ-saves person. I was a vegetarian and religious, and I had a beard and long hair. By this time, I was with a rhythm-and-blues band, and when we finished a dance in Baton Rouge a man told me someone wanted to see me outside. I went out, and there were all these guys. I guess they didn't like my clothes or my hair. One kicked me in the stomach and one in the back. They kicked me and beat me, and took my tenor and threw it as far as they could. I blacked out, and when I came to I went to the police, and the policeman said, 'Nigger, if you don't get outa here, we're going to finish you off.' I went back to New Orleans, where my friend Melvin Lastie loaned me an alto saxophone that belonged to his brother, and I went home and started playing the alto again."

When he was nineteen, Coleman went to Los Angeles with Pee Wee Crayton's rhythm-and-blues band, and he stayed for most of the next ten years. His unique playing, already formed, alienated club owners and other musicians, and he found little work. He even had trouble sitting in. The tenor saxophonist Dexter Gordon ordered him off the bandstand, and when he attempted to play with the Clifford Brown–Max Roach band the rhythm section packed up. (He never got a chance to play with Charlie Parker, but he heard him at the Tiffany Club in Los Angeles, and decided that he sounded better on records than in the flesh.) Eventually, Coleman found musicians who could hear what he was doing, and many of them are still part of his life—Don Cherry, Charlie Haden, Billy Higgins, the trumpeter Bobby Bradford, and the drummer Ed Blackwell. In 1958, the late Lester Koenig, who owned Contemporary Records, recorded Coleman, and not long after that John Lewis, the leader of the Modern Jazz Quartet, heard Coleman play in San Francisco. Lewis was enormously impressed, and told Nesuhi Ertegun, of Atlantic Records, about him. Ertegun recorded Coleman in California, and was largely responsible for Coleman's début at the Five Spot. But weak glue held all this together. Coleman kept himself alive in Los Angeles by working as a babysitter, a porter, an elevator operator, and a stock clerk. He gave blood at four dollars a pint, and sometimes he survived on canned goods sent by his mother. Other times, he roamed the streets and had nothing to eat. He wore his hair in a croquignole, and he dressed in homemade clothes. He told Leonard Feather, "I'd go out to the San Fernando Valley and sit in with, say, Gerry Mulligan. I was staying in Watts then, and I'd have to hitchhike home. And, every time, the cops would stop me, make me assemble my horn and play it to prove it was mine. Only because I'd be coming out of territory where they wouldn't expect a black person to be." Coleman was married in 1954 and had a son, Denardo, who is a drummer. He is also, Coleman says, the best thing that happened to him in California.

Coleman is a compact, medium-sized man with a strong, gentle, handsome face. His smile is lopsided and boyish. He wears his hair in a short Afro, and various beards and mustaches periodically advance and retreat. He has the even, enclosed air of someone at peace with himself and with the world, whether he can control it or not. His voice is quiet and in the middle range, and he talks in a muffled, hesitant way. His hands are stubby and his feet are small. His friend John Snyder has studied him closely. "Ornette has a total range of face," he has said. "Sometimes the wrinkles fall off, and his face becomes tight, like a kid's. Sometimes he's all wrinkles, and he makes you feel beat, he makes you feel the worst you've ever felt. He's a magnificent dresser. When he performs, he wears specially made silk suits, but he doesn't like people looking at him. If I were to tell him that one reason people do look at him is his clothes, he'd start wearing black. Ornette is sharp in other ways. A lot of people are marble-eyed—they don't see anything. Ornette looks right inside your head. He has told me things about myself that I simply could not buy but that later turned out to be absolutely true. He is also the most generous person I've ever met. He may not say sorry or thank you, but he'll give you anything. He'll pick up a derelict, take him home, clean him up, and feed him—and not get upset when the guy walks off with something. His generosity makes *you* generous. If he called today and asked would I peddle his new tape for half a million dollars, I'd do it. And he inspires you. I've sat down and written poems after being with Ornette. You can hear Ornette's goodness in his music, and he is unfailingly kind the way he goes about it. I was a trumpeter for many years, and once he wrote out a little melodic line for me that I just couldn't get. So he played it and told me to play it with him, and I did, and it was like he was literally pulling that line out of me. His new group, Prime Time, is made up of a Buddhist, a Muslim, a punk-rocker, and his son, Denardo. He has lived with them, spent years teaching them. He's had trouble with all of them, but he's stuck by them, and now they can do anything he wants.

"Ornette's music, which is supposed to be so free, is closely organized, but his personal life, which should be organized, is chaotic. He doesn't sleep much—maybe four or five hours at a time—and his hours are anything that comes.

He doesn't seem to mind where he lives. He's had cold-water flats all over the Bowery. He lived in the Century Paramount Hotel, in midtown, for half a year. He lived in a room in my office a year. I had told him he needed a place to conduct business in, and I put shelves and a desk in a back room, and next I knew he was living there. I'd take him to look at apartments, but he was never interested. He wanted a building. He had two floors that he bought in the late sixties in a loft building on Prince Street, but the rest of the tenants finally forced him out. He had turned the bottom floor into a combination night club, recording studio, rehearsal hall, and meeting place for sympathetic musicians. Some pretty loud music was played there at all hours, and Ornette simply did not understand when his neighbors got sore. To this day, he blames their evicting him on racism.

"There is a myth about how Ornette has never made any money—that he starves. Well, sometimes he *doesn't* have any money and *is* hungry, but he's made considerable sums, usually from recording contracts. He always asks top dollar. He figures that when he plays he gives a hundred per cent and the record company should give a hundred per cent, and he's absolutely right. Once, in Paris, he was invited to accompany a French ballad singer on a recording, and he said, 'O.K., but you'll have to pay me.' They asked how much. 'Ten thousand dollars,' Ornette said. Well, they paid him, by God! Sometimes the sums he asks for enrage people. When I was handling his affairs, we dickered with one of the major labels. Ornette wanted three hundred thousand dollars. His reasoning was that there were at least a hundred countries in the world and each one would buy three thousand records—as easy as that. This gent from the record company called me up after we had given them the price, and he said some pretty horrible things. Of course, the joke is that Ornette has given away most of the money he's made."

Coleman's music involves the melodies he writes, the instrumentation he sets them in, and his own playing. His

melodies are in odd lengths and shapes, and are distinguished
for their lyrical beauty, which is often dirgelike, and for
their sheer graceful irregularity. Clear in all he writes is the
influence of Thelonious Monk, who admired Duke Ellington. Coleman generally works with a group made up of
trumpet, bass, drums, and his alto saxophone. Sometimes he
substitutes a tenor saxophone for the trumpet, and sometimes he plays with just bass and drums. He has also worked
with (and written for) a string quartet, a woodwind quin-
tet, and a symphony orchestra. In the mid-seventies, he began experimenting with Prime Time, a totally original fusion group made up of two guitarists, a Fender bassist, and
one or two drummers. Coleman's playing springs from
Charlie Parker. (He has taught himself to play highly creditable trumpet and somewhat jarring left-handed violin.)
His light, voicelike tone and timbre are similar to Parker's,
and so are his runs and rhythmic stops and starts. But Coleman uses almost no vibrato, and his melodic concept is far
freer than Parker's. He has cast aside chords and keys and
harmony and conventional tonality. His solos slide from
key to key, and he uses non-tempered notes. "The tempered
sound are going to join together someday," he has said,
"and it's going to be beautiful." His time changes continually—from a four-four beat to double time to an irregular
legato to a floating, disembodied time. At first hearing,
Coleman's music sounds obscure and perverse, as if he were
deliberately playing flat, in the wrong key, and out of time.
But after a while the listener enters his world and dons his
logic. Coleman does not improvise on a theme or a set of
chords. Instead, he will start from a series of notes, a scale,
a rhythmic cluster, an area of pitch, a mood. He seems
sometimes to improvise on himself. Coleman's solos at their
best are multilayered and hypnotic. They move melodically
with such freedom and originality and surprise that they
form an independent music. It is also close to a vocal music,
for he tries—with a variety of instrumental cries and mutters
and moans and whispers—to approximate the human voice.
He has shaped the so-called free-jazz movement almost sin-

gle-handed, but none of its members, whether they admit it or not, approach his high seriousness or his lyricism.

Coleman talks about his music in coherent bursts or in quasi aphorisms that keep spilling over into philosophy. When he first came to New York, he said this about his playing: "My melodic approach is based on phrasing, and my phrasing is an extension of how I hear the intervals and pitch of the tunes I play. There is no end to pitch. You can play flat in tune and sharp in tune. It's a question of vibration. My phrasing is spontaneous, not a style. A style happens when your phrasing hardens. Jazz music is the only music in which the same note can be played night after night but differently each time. It's the hidden things, the subconscious that lies in the body and lets you know: you feel this, you play this." He has also said, " 'Improvising' is an outdated word. I try and play a musical idea that is not being influenced by any previous thing I have played before. You don't have to learn to spell to talk. The theme you play at the start of a number is the territory, and what comes after, which may have very little to do with it, is the adventure. What goes on in my head when I improvise is like human auras. Ideas flow through me the way a child grows. I play the same logic fast or slow. I don't think about feeling, seeing, or thinking. I try to have the player and the listener have the same *sound* experience. I'm not thinking about mood or emotion. Emotion should come *into* you instead of going out. All those things are built into your human fibre. When I first picked up the alto saxophone, I played it the way I thought adults must play it. What I played was not something anybody had heard before, yet it was valid. I'm still doing that. Only, I've had to package it."

John Snyder has said of Coleman's playing, "Ornette would rather compose than perform. He doesn't like performing, but when he does perform he is deadly serious. He doesn't want to just make motions. He doesn't want distractions. He doesn't cover himself with a shell. He's like a sponge. He's quick to pick up the feelings of the musicians around him and to use what he is offered. He talks a lot about 'unisons.' He doesn't mean the unison of two musicians playing the same note at the same time. His unison is any group of notes that suddenly come together and have a purity of sound—a clarity, almost a ringing. He also uses the word 'harmolodic,' which he coined and which is a contraction of the words 'harmony,' 'movement,' and 'melodic.' It's his theory of music, and it has nothing to do with what they teach you in music school. I studied theory, and Ornette's is the opposite of everything they teach you. It's the sound in the instrument. It's the structure he's built around his feelings. You cannot play anything you want with Ornette. It takes the same work—more work, if anything—as playing bebop. You cannot hide in Ornette's music. You have to know his structure. It can be a scale or three notes or a little movement. It can be a tonality, a melody, a feeling, a rhythm. This structure will allow you to play, to reveal yourself on your instrument. I've come to think that about the only way to learn how to play Ornette's music is to study with him every day for seven years. Once learned, his music would free a lot of people. It lets a musician take what he is and make music with it. You go where the improvisation is. It's already there, and you explore it. The prime motivation in Ornette's music is to reach people—even though everything in it seems to indicate the opposite."